Winning Chess
Openings

Yasser Seirawan
International Grand Master

EVERYMAN CHESS

Published by Gloucester Publishers plc, formerly Everyman Publishers plc, Gloucester
Mansions, 140a Shaftesbury Avenue, London, WC2H 8HD

British Library Cataloguing-in-Publication Data
A catalogue record for this book is available from the British Library.

ISBN 1 85744 349 7

Distributed in North America by The Globe Pequot Press, P.O Box 480, 246 Goose Lane,
Guilford, CT 06437-0480

All other sales enquiries should be directed to Everyman Chess, Gloucester Mansions,
140a Shaftesbury Avenue, London, WC2H 8HD

Tel: 020 7539 7600   Fax: 020 7379 4060
Email: info@everymanchess.com
Website: www.everymanchess.com

Everyman is the registered trade mark of Random House Inc. and is used in this work
under license from Random House Inc.

EVERYMAN CHESS SERIES (formerly Cadogan Chess)
Chief Advisor: Garry Kasparov
Commissioning editor: Byron Jacobs
Cover design by Horatio Monteverde

Printed and bound in Great Britain by Biddles Ltd, *www.biddles.co.uk*

Contents

Acknowledgments

To begin with, I'd like to thank the good folks at Microsoft Press for their continued support in publishing chess books. The previous books in the Microsoft Press Winning Chess series have been reprinted many times and this, the fifth book in the series, would certainly not have come into being without the vision of Kim Fryer and Casey Doyle. My editors, Carl Siechert and Saul Candib, saw their chess skills ramp up, but it is their editing that makes this book so readable. *Inside Chess* Editor Mike Franett provided further backup. He has been my literary "roof"—Russian for protection—for well over a decade. Thanks go to Michael Moore, Microsoft's in-house photographer, for making me smile when shooting my picture—simply by saying "Say stock-split!"

The materials for this book were compiled from nearly three decades of my own chess experience. My chess teachers, trainers, and opponents were all there to help my learning process. Often their lessons were harsh, but "…the struggling young artist improves as he suffers." Special thanks go to my wife, Yvette Nagel Seirawan, who created the diagrams, read my drafts, and put up with me for months—even on vacations—while I wrote this book. I must also make special mention of Karl Schoffstoll, who shared his enthusiasm for the openings covered and put them into practice himself. His trust was encouraging, and yes, he gained rating points.

Finally, I'd like to thank my chess friends who, through the modern miracle of e-mail, provided games, materials, and information. They include Carl Haessler, Charlie Kipp, Michael Bateman, Larry Tamarkin, and several hundred chess enthusiasts who sent me personal anecdotes and opening suggestions. What can I say? Without you all this work would be poorer and would never have happened. Thank you.

Yasser Seirawan
Seattle, Washington

Introduction

Most books have a story, and this one is no different. The Microsoft Press Winning Chess book series has inspired a large number of letters from my readers to me and to Microsoft Press. Before I continue, I'd like to offer sincere thanks to each and every one of you who took the time to write a letter! They are most appreciated. Most of your letters asked Microsoft Press to continue publishing more books in the series. Through your letters, dear readers, I earned a yummy lunch and the question "Could further titles be added to the series?"

Since book four, *Winning Chess Brilliancies*, I'd had three years to think about that question and I heartily recommended two further titles: *Winning Chess Endings* and *Winning Chess Openings*. I was very enthusiastic about an endings book because I've been carrying around thoughts for many years about how endings should be presented. This is an awkward area to study, but it remains one of the most important aspects of the game. After all, what good is it to work like a dog to establish an advantage when you can't capitalize upon your efforts?

Telling a student, "Study the ending!"—even in my sternest voice—doesn't do that much good. Most endgame books are plainly boring! The way the material has been presented, such endgame books serve as excellent aids for getting to sleep! I felt that a new approach was called for and I eagerly presented my ideas to Microsoft Press.

"And what about an opening book?" I was asked. Well yes, there was a huge problem here also. Most beginning players pound away in the opening with little rhyme or reason. Endgames are rare for such players and middle game and opening wipeouts are the rule of the day. "Well why not start there?" asked my acquisitions editor, Kim Fryer. Why not indeed? The problem was that I was much further along with my thoughts about an endings book than an openings one. Like a misplayed combination, somehow I seemed to have transposed moves!

My publishers seemed quite concerned for those lost souls who were struggling their way through their opening losses. "Let's get them through the opening first," seemed to be the sentiment. Book five was destined to be an opening book. The first book, *Play Winning Chess*, was intended as an all-purpose primer—an introduction to the vast world of chess. Books two and three, *Winning Chess Tactics* and *Winning Chess Strategies*, taught tricks and plans and could easily be read out of turn. Book four, *Winning Chess Brilliancies*, was a different sort of work. *Brilliancies* could be appreciated best by being read last. In *Brilliancies*, all the lessons of the previous works were woven together.

For *Winning Chess Openings*, the publishers wanted another work that could be read out of turn. This work is written for as broad an audience as the original *Play Winning Chess*. While *Openings* focuses upon chess openings, readers will recognize the same lessons and the same principles expounded in all the previous books. Don't expect this book to solve all your chess problems. Instead, expect it to act as a signpost on your road to development as a player.

Now came my problems. Firstly my research confirmed my fears. While there are thousands of books on the openings, I couldn't find one that took the approach I've taken with this book. "What's wrong with that?" you might ask. As a chess grandmaster, I'm constantly amazed to discover (or rather, rediscover) the truth of grandmaster Victor Kortchnoi's statement, "In chess there is nothing new under the sun." A brilliant combination? Stunning opening idea? An ending strategy? Sure enough, your "original" concept was "*first* tried in Berlin in 1866 by... and tried again in the 1938 USSR team tournament in Odessa by..."

It bears repeating that chess is 1400 years old and that our ancestors were some pretty clever people. Not to mention the folks still kicking today. It seems all but impossible to "discover" something new in chess. As for chess opening books, why, the majority of chess books are written about the openings! Failing to discover a chess book that takes the same approach as this work is perplexing. And what is so novel about the approach of this book? Why nothing more than reciting my very own experiences of what I did right and wrong! Shocking, right?

When I speak to my grandmaster colleagues about their early lessons, I'm astonished to discover how many "identical steps" we took together. Virtually all of my colleagues committed the same errors and discovered or were taught the truths in this book. So why not teach others based on the experience of myself and other elite grandmasters?

The reasons opposing this approach are surprising. Many grandmasters are embarrassed by their earliest efforts. Indeed, they want to forget about these opening losses as quickly as possible. Instead, wonderful myths are created for adoring fans, like "Grandmaster such-and-such learned chess while nursing from his mother. Our hero cast an eye at the board, reached out, and found the winning move that the greatest players of the time couldn't discover without weeks of thought…" Believe me, this nonsense gets spewed through endless pages of chess literature. Unfortunately, the heroes in these works tend to encourage this type of rubbish. "Well, that's not exactly how it happened," our blushing hero would state. "You see, it actually took me a number of reflections to refute the analysis of the former World Champion. You see, my school work and karate studies got in my way and…"

No one likes to remember the first time they burned their fingers on a wicked candle flame. It is the very rare and careful person who hasn't burnt himself or herself. Indeed, it took me a few dozen outings to respect the candle's flame. I really enjoyed playing with the candle's wax on my fingertips. Am I so different? I don't think so!

So speaking as a chess grandmaster, allow me to recite my own first-hand experiences of my failings as a beginner and how the flame of defeat helped guide me in the openings. It is my hope that you will recognize yourself in these passages. Smile to yourself when you see an old pothole that rattled your hubcaps. Before too long, you might discover that a future pothole awaits your entry. If you take my own experiences to heart, you might just miss one that got me.

I've tried to present the material in the order that it was taught to me. In Chapters One and Two, you'll see the stunning chess opening discoveries that I thought of "on my own." My games weren't always pretty, and you'll soon appreciate what a poor player I was. Only after working with experienced chess players—who became my chess teachers—did I learn the classical King Pawn and classical Queen Pawn openings. These are explained in Chapters Three and Four. They are difficult chapters because they both have a "main line" through the chapter. At every single move, a different idea or variation is looked at! This is quite vexing because it seems that we'll never wind our way through the main line. Why did I present this information on the classical openings in this style? Because that's exactly how it was presented to me!

When my teachers took me through the classical openings, they didn't whip through the first dozen moves and proudly state, "So that, Yasser, is the Queen's Gambit Declined!" On the contrary, they encouraged me to question every move, including the first one. I wasn't being asked to memorize an opening; I was taught to understand the logic of the move. Having a young inquiring mind, I wanted to know why a move was good or bad. These questions were always answered, provided that I properly framed my questions according to opening principles. I soon learned that nearly every logical move had an opening name! Thus I learned a large number of names. The "Fried Liver Attack" was a favorite, whereas the "Nimzo-Indian, Rubinstein Variation" hardly rolls of the tongue. Thus, I teach the classical openings in the same manner: by questioning every move and looking at the alternatives while trying to stay on a main line.

Modern openings and defenses are dealt with differently. In Chapters Five and Six, I no longer follow a main line. Instead I describe each defense in its own section. In this way, you can judge each defense on its own merits and failings. I've made judgements on nearly all the defenses given, and I leave it up to you to discover if I'm right or wrong.

After I learned the classics and the principles, it seemed to me that a fair number of modern defenses violate the principles. They do. Principles are only guides; they are not rules. Do not cling to principles as the sole answer to a given position. They are there to stimulate you to think up the right move or plan.

The amount of theory of chess openings is overwhelming. It seemed that I was always a step behind my opponent on the latest opening moves. (And yes, my karate lessons were getting in the way of my chess studies.) There was only one solution: to try to avoid the sharpest theoretical variations and instead create a solid hiding place for my King. Once that had been done, I turned to dealing with the center, finding a plan, and conducting possible attacks. These lessons are contained in Chapters Seven, Eight, and Nine. Beginning players will always get wiped out by more experienced opponents. One of the major reasons is that the King lacks protection. These chapters are specifically designed to prevent all further short losses. You'll be taught to have a safe King and you will be well supplied with the insights of classical and modern openings and defenses.

Throughout the book, I've diligently tried to state the names of the openings, defenses, variations, and attacks that I describe. This has led to a number of awkward moments. The word *opening* often refers to what White is doing and *defense* refers to what Black is doing, but sometimes a favored variation as White is tried with the colors reversed. "I like this opening as White, so I'll play it as Black!" Of course, the converse is also true. A difficult one is the King's Indian Defense, a line of defense favored by a number of World Champions when playing the Black pieces. But if White adopts the King's Indian Defense setup, is it a King's Indian Defense or a King's Indian Opening? In such cases the term *reversed* is often used.

Although the words *opening, defense, variation*, and *attack* are often used interchangeably, I've tried to reserve *opening* for White's play and *defense* for Black's play. With a game that's 1400 years old, expect some strange nomenclature to have been incorporated along the way.

As always, I wish you the very best of success in your endeavors and I hope that this book will stimulate you into buying further books that are more specific about the openings and defenses that you might enjoy.

CHAPTER ONE

Early Days

Take a look at Diagram 1, the starting position of a chess game. It is the most complicated position in chess. Believe me. Grandmaster David Bronstein, who drew a match for the World Chess Championship in 1951, oftentimes would come to a major tournament game and sit in wonderment staring at this very position. He once spent over 50 minutes on his very first move! And what on earth was this chess genius, this titan, this virtual co-champion of the entire chess world thinking about?

"I was wondering what to play," David said.

Is the starting position really that complex? The answer is more complicated than a simple yes or no. And the complexity grows as the student learns more! When I was playing my first games of chess, I was absolutely certain what was the best move. (Of course, I was dead wrong.) Now as an International Grandmaster, I find myself weighing the pros and cons of the

multiple openings I play and I try to imagine which one would give my opponent the most discomfort. As a player's style of play matures, the player's choice of openings goes through subtle changes. When a pet favorite that used to bring home the victories is no longer scoring as well, a shift often proves successful. After trying out different formations, the player makes more changes. Thus the starting position becomes ever

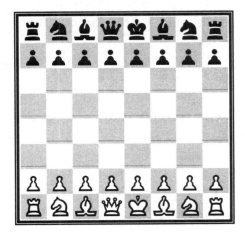

DIAGRAM 1.

1

more complex as an experienced player starts to seriously juggle the possible openings and defenses.

Some chess positions with a mere half-dozen pieces seem unsolvable. The starting position with all 32 pieces on the board becomes overwhelming. There are so many moves to think about, and every one of our pieces cries out for attention. It can lead to paralysis of the mind.

"Move me!" shouts the e2-pawn. "I'm Bobby Fischer's favorite move!"

"Look," says our King's Rook, "I'm cramped and boxed in. Get me into the action and I'll show you why I'm called a cannon!"

"Don't be silly!" states our noble Queen. "I'm the most powerful of all! Bring me into the battle. The entire board will bow before me."

As I started to play my earliest games, a jumble of voices confused my poor brain. Such a chorus of demands, my goodness! Willy-nilly, I'd choose my favorite piece of the moment. The chosen piece gets to move, jump, or stumble around until the lucky chosen one gets removed from the board. I thought, "What a pity! Just when things were getting good! Well, let's see… That plan was working really well! If only my poor fellow hadn't been captured. Bad luck that. Well, there is another one, let's use it!" And off I would go, until the newly chosen gets slaughtered. How unlucky our pawns and pieces seem to be. "What's this? A check? How on earth did my King get checked? Looks like his majesty has to take a stroll…"

If the above thoughts reflect your early efforts, you now realize that your despairs have been shared. *I did the very same thing.* These early thoughts of victory accurately describe how I got clobbered. Those early losses came quickly and furiously! While most of my very earliest games are thankfully lost to posterity, I remember a number of them quite well. I still recall that some of these losses really hurt. I was so certain of the correctness of my approach, and I'd stubbornly cling to my earliest beliefs. In fact, I was so stubborn, I'm rather disbelieving that I actually became a grandmaster!

Copying the Opponent

The following is the earliest game that I can recall.

Yasser Seirawan versus Unknown, Unfriendly Foe

Follow my moves in silent fascination.

1.d3?

Why this mistaken move? Actually I wasn't sure what to do. Of the chorus this one little pawn seemed to cry loudest. I make this "pass" move as I had already "discovered" a brilliant strategy, which I will soon reveal.

1...d5

My more experienced opponent makes a very reasonable move.

2.d4?

This was my brilliant discovery! I would merely duplicate my opponent's move, thereby negating the need for any thought on my part. Clever, no? I would keep a careful eye on my opponent's moves, deduce an error in his plan, and then deviate at the critical moment to score a brilliant victory.

2...e5!?

My opponent tries a speculative gambit.

3.e4?

Continuing to ape my opponent, my clever strategy begins to unfold.

3...Bg4?

My opponent blunders by putting a Bishop in capture (the French term *en prise* is the chess vernacular, but I was too inexperienced to have learned this term) to my Queen.

4.dxe5?

Of course, I was attracted to the possibility of duplicating my opponent's move with 4.Bg5, but already my natural talent began to expose itself. Somehow I "sensed" the critical moment to deviate had come. My opponent's move had to be an error and I took advantage of the moment to grab a central pawn. I never considered the best move, 4.Qxg4, for a single moment. At that time I didn't have a complete grasp of how my pieces were supposed to move.

4...Bb4+?

With this eye-popping move, my opponent announced Checkmate! Happily my opponent began explaining to me how his Bishops were scissoring my position and that my King had no moves. He said I shouldn't be upset by this premature loss, because I was his *fourth* victim of this devastating trap.

Diagram 2 shows the final position from this game. Today I can only stare at this position with open-mouthed horror. White isn't checkmated at all! By playing any of the moves 5.c3, 5.Nc3, 5.Nd2, 5.Bd2, or 5.Qd2, the check to my King is stopped. Of course, White will lose his Queen and probably the game, so let us quickly turn the page!

Now is the time for the first critical lesson from this book:

Write down the moves to all your games and save your game scores.

Oftentimes you will play quick games or five-minute chess. I can only encourage you to record these games as best you can. Try to record the moves as they are made, but if this is inconvenient, try to reconstruct the game afterward and make a *written record*. I improved my play enormously by doing this simple exercise and charting my own progress.

The importance of this lesson and its impact on my understanding of chess didn't manifest itself for several months. First it was necessary to lose dozens of games.

DIAGRAM 2.

Cannon Fire

Another game that typified my earliest "style" was demonstrated in the following encounter.

Yasser Seirawan versus Known Unfriendly Fiend

In viewing Diagram 1, the starting position, I imagined myself to be Napoleon—a fine general in charge of an army ready to defy all opposition for their commander. The air is fresh and clean as the individual units stamp their fury, anxious to engage the enemy. Being a commander concerned for each individual unit, I decide to lob the enemy using my cannons! Of course, a littie tenderizing of the enemy with cannons is just the right strategy before sending in the cavalry. From the starting position, I formed an image of my Rooks as cannons. They were born to fire their salvos up the files and along the ranks. Backed by my fantasy of commanding an army, I make use of my Hollywood movie-viewing experiences and come to the only possible conclusion: "Light the cannons!"

1.h4?

This was my favorite opening move!

1...d5

With the advantage of many victories backing his choice, my opponent makes a particularly powerful move.

2.Rh3?

I bring my cannons into battle right away so that the enemy ranks would be softened up.

2...Bxh3!

This truly excellent move should have been discouraging. Not to be deterred, I conjure up yet another fabulous effort.

3.a4??

This mistake gets a second question mark. After blundering my Rook I should have played 3.Nxh3, capturing the Black Bishop as compensation.

3...e5?

Complacency born from the firm knowledge of previous victories leads to a mistake. Black should retreat his endangered Bishop.

4.Ra3??

I had a dim awareness that this mind-boggling move was a mistake, but, what the heck, consistency is the hallmark of genius and I was determined to have my cannons blaze away!

4...Bxa3!

What is up with this jerk anyway? He hasn't missed a trick! Now that my Rooks have disappeared, a sudden fear grips my heart. My h4-pawn is open to attack by the Black Queen. Feeling sympathy for the valiant foot soldier, I see no reason to allow its capture. Yes! I see the point of my play clearly now. First I play:

5.h5?

If he misses my point I will play 6.h6 and 7.hxg7 and gxh8=Q winning...

Diagram 3 shows how I would lose many, many games. It seemed like a cruel fate, but my cannons were hardly ever around after the first dozen moves!

By now you should be getting the idea of what a truly hopeless chess player I was when I started out. Later I would create my own philosophy that went like this: "Every mistake should be repeated at least once. In that way the original mistake could be confirmed." How could you be sure if you made a mistake based upon a single loss? So now you're beginning to see that I was a hopeless, *stubborn* chess player!

This brings me to the second critical lesson:

Believe in your own ideas.

Not all your ideas will be bright ones. In fact, you'll probably have ten false trails for every true one you find. Fine! So be it! But believe in your ideas. Cling to them stubbornly. Give up on them slowly, only after severe trial and tribulations. If you keep getting clobbered,

DIAGRAM 3.

then seek an adjustment, but don't be afraid to play your own moves. They might be bad, but you'll learn a lot faster playing your own moves instead of mimicking others. Adjust your ideas by the results of your own practice.

At this early point in my career, I still hadn't learned the first critical lesson, but I sure had mastered the second. I knew my ideas were clever; they just needed some slight fine tuning.

After about 30 losses of "cannon positioning," I discovered my real powerhouse: my Queen. A whole new array of losses awaited me.

Queen Raid

After determining that my cannon-fire ideas weren't doing the job, a careful rethink of my opening approach was necessary. This was a critical phase of my chess development. It seemed that chess was far too difficult for my poor mind. Was trying to get better worth getting stomped by my friends?

All chess players at one time in their very early career are struck by this telling question. Many decide that, indeed, chess isn't their shtick. Fortunately for me, a serendipitous outside influence played a crucial role at this phase in my development. My interest was rekindled when America's own Robert James (Bobby) Fischer defeated the Soviet Union's Boris Spassky for the World Chess Championship in 1972. It was a heady moment for chess players around the world, and for American chess players in particular.

While most Americans were undoubtedly proud of their new champion, I had a question: "How could Bobby be champion? He didn't beat me!"

Renewing myself, I applied the formidable powers of my young mind to my opening strategy. Carefully penetrating the mysterious veil of the chess pieces, I deduced something wonderful and extraordinary: My Queen is the most powerful piece on the board!

My fault had been not to develop it quickly enough. How simple and obvious: My Queen was a natural-born bully! All that was necessary was to introduce it into the game as early as possible.

This faulty strategy is one of the most insidious pitfalls in chess! I fell into it headlong, as *every untrained beginner has done!* The problem, dear reader, is simply this: *The Queen Raid strategy worked!* My results against my circle of chess friends immediately improved. Two early examples of victorious play convinced me that I was on the right track.

Yasser Seirawan versus Known Unfriendly Fiend

This game begins with a good opening move—played with the completely wrong strategy in mind. The intention should be to grab control of the center, not to make room for my Queen! Controlling the center certainly wasn't my intention.

1.e4 e5

This is the classical answer and a good move. Even beginners occasionally find good moves!

2.Qh5?

This was my "new and improved" idea. As the new neighborhood bully, my Queen would knock heads together.

2...g6??

My opponent seizes the opportunity to attack my Queen, but overlooks my real threat.

3.Qxe5+

Simply brilliant! My Queen spears Black's position. Now Black's cannon (Rook) will be eaten.

3...Qe7

Black copies my plan of bringing out the Queen. My turn!

4.Qxh8

My Queen happily munches the trapped Rook.

4...Qxe4+

What's this? The capture presents danger, but I can block the check and my Rook is safe.

5.Ne2

With this good move, I develop a piece and block the check.

5...Qxc2(?)

What a sly devil my opponent is! Now he is conducting his own raid. My goodness, how do I defend the threat of 6...Qxc1 Checkmate? A sudden panic overcomes me, followed by a sigh of relief. No! My brilliant fifth move with my Knight protects my c1-Bishop! Happily, I continue my own raid.

6.Qxg8

In a greedy (and good, I might add) move, a mighty Knight is slaughtered. My marauding Queen is picking apart Black's army. Isn't chess easy and fun? I'm sure such gleeful thoughts were printed on my face.

6...Nc6

Black makes a good move and develops a piece. Now, at the position shown in Diagram 4, I had a real think about what to do next.

By this time I was experienced enough to make a realization. I had a won position! I've grabbed enough loot—a Rook and a Knight—to have a big edge. Do I need to win more material? The h7-pawn is a very tempting grab as my raid *on the Kingside* would be completed. However, Black's Queen is quite worrying and I must pay attention so that I don't blow my win. Resisting my strong inclination to play 7.Qxh7, I instead decide to attack Black's raiding Queen.

7.Na3!

In another surprisingly good move, and without understanding what I

DIAGRAM 4.

9

was doing, I've developed a Knight with tempo. That is, I mobilize one of my pieces and attack Black's Queen at the same time. The realization that "Black's Queen will have to move because I've attacked the Queen!" planted a seed that would take root and grow. This seed would lead me to reevaluate my new Queen strategy.

7...Qa4

This is a move I could fully understand and appreciate. Beginners like myself who have discovered the Queen strategy try to throw the Queen right into the middle of the battle. When the Queen is attacked, my natural reaction is to return the favor at once! As my Knight attacks Black's Queen, the Queen responds by attacking my White Knight. Just what I would do! My admiration for my opponent's play was growing.

I looked at the captured pieces to restore my confidence. I'm still a Rook and Knight ahead! I love what has just taken place. I've gobbled up nearly half of my opponent's army and I had just attacked Black's Queen. It felt so good that I only considered two moves: taking the h7-pawn or the move I chose.

8.b3!

Playing 8.Qxh7 was nearly irresistible. But attacking Black's Queen had brought such pleasure previously, I just couldn't resist. This time, the thought behind the move was correct. My c1-Bishop protects the Knight and the Black Queen is given another boot.

8...Qb4

Black tries to keep his Queen as close to the action as possible. Once more my opponent had completed the very move I would have played. At this stage of my chess career, I rarely saw more than one move ahead. My move always seemed to be spur of the moment and at this moment I was on a roll. Black's Queen has had to *react* to my previous moves. Without hesitation I plunked down my next move.

9.Nc2?

What joy, attacking Black's Queen again! My pieces are being brought into play and the game is won. (With the benefit of 25 years' hindsight, 9.Nc4 is a far better move.)

9...Qc5?

I thought this move to be an excellent retort because it follows the reasoning, "When attacked, counter with an attack of your own." In fact, this move just loses. While Black is quite lost because of his material deficit, a better choice is 9...Qe4 to get out of harm's way.

Diagram 5 shows the position as we come to one of the proudest moments of my early career: my first *combination*. Of course, I didn't call my next move a combination (I didn't know what the word meant); it was simply wonderful.

10.Ba3!

I continue harassing the Black Queen. This was the very first move I considered, but because Black's last move attacked my c2-Knight, I was going to give up on this move when I spotted—by sheer luck—that the move has a deeper purpose then merely attacking Black's Queen.

10...Qxc2

Played with a near yelp of delight, my fiendish opponent wasn't about to be chivalrous and say, "Look here young Yasser, you've overlooked my threat to capture your Knight. Why don't you reconsider?"

11.Qxf8 Checkmate

This stunning dénouement had an extraordinary effect on my enjoyment of chess. I was as dumbfounded as my opponent, who could only stare in helpless reflection at the final position. I had actually anticipated two moves in a row. I had consciously sacrificed a Knight in order to win back a Bishop!

DIAGRAM 5.

11

You must understand that at this stage of my chess understanding, captures came only as a result of an oversight by myself or my opponent or due to a mutually recognized immediate trade of pieces. Sometimes captures were ignored all together. This little trick caused a near explosion in my cranium. It was possible to sacrifice a piece with a higher purpose in mind!

From this victory I deduced all the wrong lessons. Now I was more convinced then ever that I was close to solving the mystery of chess and what to do in the opening. I now believed that *the key to victory was developing the Queen early* in order to raid the flanks, and that in this way an *early checkmate was possible*. As experience would prove, I was completely wrong.

At this time, most of my games were usually lopsided affairs where my opponents would delight in taking my entire army first, before checkmating my King! That was simply the way it was done. Most of the time, I was checkmated without the aid of any of my pieces or pawns on the board. This was another reason why the victory just described resonated so loudly: *Black's very own pieces blocked Black's King from escaping.*

Thus I came to arguably the greatest pitfall for *all beginners*: an overwhelming fascination with the Queen's power. My concern for its wellbeing became so great that the game ceased to be interesting when Queens were traded or—worst of all—lost! Let's look at one more of my typical victories from this period. First I must confess that I wasn't entirely comfortable with White. I was unsure if I should play 1.e4 and 2.Qh5 or 2.Qf3, 1.d4 and 2.Qd3, or 1.c4 and 2.Qb3. My rate of success was pretty good with all three tries but I was dy-no-mite with the Black pieces! Witness the following epic.

Known Fiend versus Yasser Seirawan

My chess-playing friends and I fell into a pattern of playing certain opening formations that we liked. My friends liked this move because they had seen Bobby Fischer play it. None of us knew why. My answer would come like lightning.

1.e4 d5

This is actually not a bad opening move, and it goes by the name of the *Scandinavian Defense*—although at the time I didn't know that.

2.exd5 Qxd5

I was already in my glory. My Queen had been introduced into the game with a wide-open field. Now I'd ferret out a weakness to capture.

3.Nc3

This good move attacks my Queen and forces it to move again. This move hadn't yet made an impression upon my young mind, as it had always been my intention to play with my Queen.

3...Qe6+?

My Queen is misplaced here and will be forced to move again. The opening theory of the Scandinavian Defense is that 3...Qa5, keeping Black's Queen out of danger, is the recommended move. My choice of move is typical of beginning players. The expression "patzer (weak player) sees a check, patzer plays a check" is appropriate for this move.

4.Be2 Qg6

I've discovered a potential weakness in White's g2-pawn and immediately take aim, as shown in Diagram 6.

5.Bb5+?

Played in true patzer style, this move ignores the obvious threat to capture the g2-pawn. White should defend the g2-pawn by 5.Bf3. In this case White would look to play Ng1-e2-f4 in order to attack Black's Queen.

5...c6!

DIAGRAM 6.

The venerable grandmaster Victor Kortchnoi would describe this very good move as "a blind hand finding a seed." I block the check to my King while returning the threat to White's Bishop.

6.Ba4?

White again overlooks the threat to the g2-pawn; the retreat 6.Bf1 is the best move.

6...b5

I seize the opportunity to attack White's Bishop once again. A better move is 6...Qxg2, following through on the planned raid.

7.Nxb5?

White sacrifices a Knight for doubtful compensation. After 7.Bb3 Qxg2 8.Qf3 White could have limited his losses to a pawn.

7...Qxg2!　　　　**8.Nc7+**

White happily forks King and Rook. After 8.Qf3 Qxf3 9.Nxf3 cxb5 10.Bxb5+ Bd7, Black would have a clear advantage in force as he has won a Knight for a pawn. Of course, at this point in my career, this advantage was by no means decisive!

8...Kd8　　　　**9.Nxa8 Qxh1**

As shown in Diagram 7, the Rook trade leaves White in a desperate situation, as his King will soon be exposed.

10.Kf1 Bh3+!　　**11.Ke1??**

This terrible move loses the game almost at once. After the forced 11.Ke2 Bg4+ 12.f3 (the move my opponent had overlooked) 12...Qg2+ 13.Kd3 Bf5+ 14.Kc3, White's King is trotting around the board, but it is still a fight.

11...Qxg1+　　**12.Ke2 Bg4+**
13.f3 Bxf3+!

DIAGRAM 7.

This fine move separates White's Queen from the protection of the King.

14.Kxf3 Qd1+

At the position shown in Diagram 8, White resigns.

Unhappy about the loss of his Queen and with no ambitions for the remaining pieces, my opponent gave up.

A number of similar victories convinced me of the correctness of my new approach. Developing my

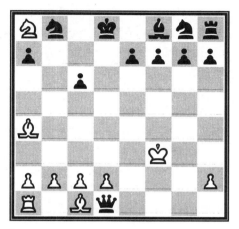

DIAGRAM 8.

Queen as quickly as possible gave chances for an early knockout raid. It was certainly more successful than my Cannon Opening!

Destroying the Queen Raid

It was at this point that I discovered a coffeehouse in Seattle's University District called The Last Exit on Brooklyn. The chess players who met here were far more experienced players than my usual circle of friends. It was here that my Queen Raid approach received a number of nasty setbacks. The harshest lesson was the following game, which left a deep impression.

Yasser Seirawan versus Known Experienced Player

This was a big game for me. I was playing an experienced adult chess player and was anxious to prove my newfound understanding of opening play. My opening had but one aim: creating an avenue for my Queen to develop.

1.e4 e5

Black responds with the *Classical King Pawn Defense*. I didn't know the defense had a name, but it was a standard counter in my circle of friends.

2.Qh5?

Of course I was very happy to play this mistake, allowing my Queen to immediately begin its attack. Naturally, I'm poised to grab Black's e5-pawn.

2...Nc6

This reaction put the brakes to my plan. Black easily defends my one and only threat. It was time to create another.

3.Bc4

White threatens 4.Qxf7, which is well known as the *Scholar's Mate*. The term wasn't known to me, but the threat certainly was! How would my experienced opponent react?

3...g6!

In a good move, Black blocks my threat to the f7-pawn and attacks my Queen as well. Undeterred, I retreat my Queen and renew the same threat.

4.Qf3

Thus far I was very proud of my play. Aggressive from the start, I had held the initiative and was really taking the game to my opponent! Surely he felt the same way too?

4...Nf6!

Black calmly blocks my threat to the f7-pawn and develops another piece. Now I fully concentrated to find something creative. After some intense thought, I found a nifty idea.

5.Qb3?

As I was about to discover, this was a mistake. At the time, I really liked this move because it fit perfectly with my newfound knowledge. The f7-pawn is attacked yet again—how brilliant I am!—and my Queen is perfectly positioned to grab the b7-pawn if opportunity allows. Yes indeed, things are really going my way!

5...Nd4!

Black's excellent response is one my young mind didn't appreciate. Of course Black's Knight attacks my Queen, but my opponent apparently hadn't realized my threat so I eagerly seize the opportunity to capture a pawn with check, as shown in Diagram 9.

6.Bxf7+

I was certainly proud of this move. My opponent is forced to move his King, I'm a pawn up, and I'd be victorious after just a few more stern moves. I was a bit perplexed that my esteemed opponent was not perturbed by the need to move his King.

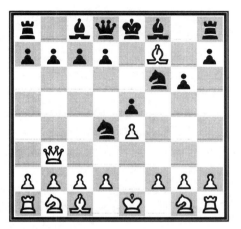

DIAGRAM 9.

6...Ke7   7.Qc4

In the far recesses of my mind a doubt appeared. I was surprised that I didn't have an immediate checkmate. What a pity that 7.Qe6 isn't checkmate! In that case, either the d7-pawn or the d4-Knight would capture my Queen. My first idea was to play 7.Qb4+. (My second check in a row! I would be on a roll.) But after 7...Kxf7, I'd lose my Bishop and my Queen would be under attack.

7...b5!

Where did this unexpected move come from? Wasn't I the one making all the threats? Black's move attacking my Queen forces me to give up the protection of my Bishop.

8.Qc5+ Kxf7

I was very sorry to see the capture of my valiant Bishop. After all, this Bishop had forced Black's King to move. Now my hand faltered. I had intended to grab Black's e5-pawn when my attention was drawn to my c2-pawn. My goodness! After 9.Qxe5 Nxc2+ 10.Kd1 Nxa1, my King will have been checked and I would lose a Rook.

9.Qc3

A rather painful retreat, but I couldn't allow the capture of the c2-pawn and my Queen had to move.

9...Bb4!

Black unleashes another powerful and unexpected move! I had been warned that my opponent was a "good player." But this apparently wasn't true; my opponent has just blundered a Bishop. My hand reached out to grab the Bishop but faltered. Why? Well, my Queen protects my c2-pawn and if I take the Bishop... Yikes! It dawns on me that with 10.Qxb4 Nxc2+, my King and Queen are forked by a Knight. I'd lose my Queen. This means that I can't capture Black's Bishop. What's even worse is that my Queen is attacked again and I must move. I revise my evaluation of my opponent: He is good! He had just set a trap of two moves. He had actually *anticipated* my move. How on earth had he figured that out? Now my harried Queen must move again, but I can't allow the capture of my c2-pawn.

10.Qd3 d5!

At last, a mistake! My opponent has missed my threat of c2-c3 forking Bishop and Knight. Now I'd get the chance to win back the piece I'd lost. Finally, for the last time, my hand faltered yet again. Surely my crafty opponent would not overlook losing a piece? Right, that was the trick! Black's last move introduces the threat of 11...dxe4, winning a pawn, and worse, attacking my Queen yet again!

11.exd5

Fearful of 11...dxe4, I couldn't allow my pawn to be captured. I still had my ambitions. Given the chance, the move c2-c3 would win back my piece.

11...Bf5!

I couldn't believe what had just happened. With another fine attacking move, my Queen was again under attack and had to move. My game is terrible. Black's pieces are buzzing about the board and all I have developed is my Queen. The Queen, which I thought was a bully, was getting pushed around. With a heavy heart I abandoned the defense of my c2-pawn and accepted the loss of a Rook.

12.Qg3

I recall being quite proud of this move. I realized that 12.Qe3 Nxc2+ would fork my King and Queen. Unblinking, my opponent immediately attacked my Queen yet again!

12...Nh5!

I couldn't believe my opponent had resisted the temptation to play 12...Nxc2+, which I evaluated as winning. So why this move? Once again my Queen would have to move, but where? Take a look at

DIAGRAM 10.

Diagram 10 and you'll realize my discomfort. Nearly all the squares available to my Queen are guarded!

13.Qxe5

I avoid stepping into the same ...Nd4xc2+ Knight fork, and I console myself with the thought that I have wiped out a pawn. I saw Black's next move but there was nothing I could do.

13...Re8!

By pinning my Queen to my King, the cannon had never seemed more powerful! Knowing my Queen was lost, I captured the Rook.

14.Qxe8+ Qxe8+

What a disaster! My Queen is captured and my King is checked. Flustered by the suddenness of my losing position, I found my last bad move.

15.Kd1? Bxc2 Checkmate

My experienced opponent didn't bother to announce checkmate and instead left it to me to find a move. (See Diagram 11, on the next page.) With my hand on my King and a puzzled expression, I tried moving my King to a few squares. When I couldn't find a square, I looked at my opponent. He gave me a knowing smile and then said, "Checkmate."

DIAGRAM 11.

This game left me shaking my head. After I returned home, I went over the game very carefully and came to some startling conclusions:

■ Instead of being a bully, *my Queen had actually been chased around the board,* having to respond to every threat against it.

■ While my opponent was developing his forces, I was falling behind. The final position, shown in Diagram 11, was a forceful reminder of how lopsided the victory was. Not a single White piece had been developed. I had played 15 moves and nearly all my pieces were on their original squares. The only two pieces that had managed to make it into the game, my Queen and Bishop, had been captured.

This sparked a whole new way of thinking and I discovered another principle:

While an early Queen Raid against a <u>beginner</u> is effective, a Queen Raid will not work against an experienced opponent who knows how to coordinate pieces.

Chess coaches all over the world understand this truism! Beginners are very vulnerable to Queen Raids. Once they learn how to coordinate their pieces and pawns and ward off an early Queen Raid, the strategy fails. The early development of the Queen is a detriment for the other pieces and the strategy boomerangs against the raider.

Danny Noble versus Allison Borngesser, 1998 National Elementary Championships

Before moving on to Chapter Two, I'd like to share the following game. During the time I spent writing this book, I received the June 1998 issue of *Northwest Chess*, the monthly publication for the Washington and Oregon State Chess Federations, which reported on the 1998 National Elementary Championships that had been held in April. National Chess Master Carl Haessler, who has been successfully teaching chess to scholastic players for years, accompanied several of his students to the 1998 Nationals and shared their successes and sorrows. Carl's report featured the following game.

1.e4 e5   2.Qh5

I look at this move with a knowing smile of understanding. How exciting! Will Black see the threat to the e5-pawn?

2...Nf6?

No, the threat is overlooked! As I've previously demonstrated, there is no reason not to protect the e5-pawn.

3.Qxe5+ Be7   4.Bc4 Nc6!

Very good. The raiding Queen is attacked and a piece is developed with tempo.

5.Qf4 O-O   6.e5?

Played in the spirit of the raiding Queen opening, White makes threats as quickly as possible. Much better is developing a piece with 6.Nc3.

6...Nxe5??

This mistake costs a Knight. As Black's f6-Knight is attacked by a pawn, it should simply move. Black's choices are 6...Ne8, which is a safe retreat, or she can move and simultaneously attack White's Queen with the ambitious 6...Nh5. If White plays 7.Qf3 or 7.Qg4, then 7...Nxe5! 8.Qxh5 Nxc4 allows Black to win back the pawn with a superior game.

7.Qxe5

Things are certainly going in White's favor. He has now won a piece and enjoys a winning position. All of this in only seven moves!

7...d6

Undeterred by the early setback of material loss, Black continues by developing a pawn with tempo. Unfortunately, this move has a drawback: The e7-Bishop is locked in behind Black's f6-Knight and d6-pawn. This is important because the only open file in the position is the e-file and the e7-Bishop is therefore misplaced. A Rook belongs on the e-file! Stronger therefore is 7...d5!, attacking White's Bishop. After 8.Be2 Bd6! White's Queen is forced to move yet again. In this case, Black is coordinating her pawns and pieces and is beginning to get some play for the lost piece.

8.Qf4 Ng4?

The idea behind the move is to play 9...Bg5, attacking White's Queen. As pointed out before, a stronger move is 8...d5! 9.Be2 Bd6, developing Black's forces with gain of time. Diagram 12 shows the current position.

9.h4?

This looks like the start of a bad idea. Is White combining a Queen Raid and a Cannon Opening? Simplest is 9.Nf3, which develops a piece and prevents a 9...Bg5 attack on White's Queen.

9...Ne5   10.h5?

This continues to waste time pursuing an attack that is going nowhere.

DIAGRAM 12.

Again, 10.Nf3 is the correct move. White's wasted moves allow Black to get back into the game.

10...Nxc4?!

Although it's not a bad move, it's not the best. Black could make White's position uncomfortable by attacking White's Queen with 10...Bg5!. The Queen is forced to move and to still lend protection to the c4-Bishop. After 10.Qe4 Re8, the e-file has been cleared with tempo and Black has developed some threats.

11.Qxc4 Be6

A fine move. While Black has mixed good and bad moves, young Allison has a fine understanding of attacking White's Queen while developing her pawns and pieces. Still, it must be pointed out that the e6-Bishop's new station occupies the e-file. Once again the move 11...d5! should have been preferred.

12.Qc3?

White continues to flounder. The Queen is getting bumped around pretty severely. It would have been better to get out of the way by 12.Qa4, or play 12.Qb5 with a potential capture of the b7-pawn. This latter move could have been expected as it neatly fits the concept of the Queen Raid. White might have been attracted to 12.Qc3? because in combination with the move h5-h6, a checkmating threat against the g7-pawn would have been created.

12...Bf6!

Black is on a roll! She attacks White's Queen yet again.

13.Qd3?

White is losing valuable time. He should play 13.d4, blocking the threat to his Queen and releasing his c1-Bishop for action.

13...Re8!

With another fine move, Black brings her Rook to the open e-file and creates a tactical threat, as shown in Diagram 13.

14.h6??

Filled with dreams of glory, White is oblivious to Black's threat. White should develop with 14.Ne2, blocking the e-file. This move is typical of inexperienced players who concentrate only on what they are doing—not what the opponent might be thinking.

DIAGRAM 13.

14...Bf5+!

A shocking double attack, the *discovered check* by the e8-Rook doesn't allow the capture of the f5-Bishop. White is forced to lose his Queen.

15.Qe2 Rxe2+   16.Nxe2 g6

Black won the game in 39 moves.

Many lessons can be drawn from the above game fragment:

- Beginning players enjoy using their big guns, their Queens and Rooks, early—often to the exclusion of all the other pieces.

- The Queen Raid is effective when threats are overlooked.

- Against a proper defense, the Queen is vulnerable to attack and is often left stranded.

CHAPTER TWO

Basic Opening Principles

Journeying often to the Last Exit coffeehouse, I found that a whole new understanding of the chess world opened up to me. By playing against experienced players, I gained a new appreciation for the game. All my opening "innovations" were being neatly refuted, and I was completely unable to survive the opening stages. I'm extremely grateful to all the chess players at the Last Exit who took pity on my poor efforts and began to dissect my opening mistakes. I'd especially like to thank Jeffrey Parsons and James Blackwood, who happily spent many hours teaching me the game's many mysteries. I soon learned the important principles of opening play. These principles were laid down as follows and they are as valid as ever:

A chess game has three phases: the opening, the middle game, and the endgame. In the opening, <u>pawns and minor pieces play the key roles</u>. The major pieces—the Queen and the Rooks—do not.

This principle brought a newfound awareness. If I was to have any chance against an experienced player, I had to learn how to use my pawns and to develop my Knights and Bishops first. I had to resist the impulse to raid with my Queen or to expect my cannons to blaze away. Of course I could not do this! Only countless telling losses made me understand this principle. My opponents at the Last Exit beat me like a drum. The word "victory" seemed to apply only to my opponent. Finally, like a stubborn mule, I chose to accept the well-worn path to chess mastery and I learned a slew of new opening ideas.

While I continued to lose many games, I was also fortunate to witness many games between strong players. One thing that confounded me was how vulnerable the King is in the opening. Time and time again a King was checkmated within 10 to 20 moves. Often a player didn't go after the win of a pawn or a piece but instead launched an all-out assault on an enemy King. This invariably happened when the victim neglected to develop his pieces. The idea that a player intentionally sacrificed material—usually a pawn—for superior development was quite charming. The concept of sacrificing material for a gain in development is called a *gambit*. This strategy instantly became one of my favorites. First I had to learn a few more opening principles.

The purpose of the opening is to get a safe King and an equal middle game.

This principle at first saddened me very much. When I sat down to play a new game of chess, I was charged. I wanted to win right away; the sooner the better! That was the purpose of my Queen Raid and I delighted whenever an opponent fell into the Scholar's Mate. It was Jeffrey who convinced me of the correctness of this principle. He asked me how often I had checkmated one of my beginner friends in a Scholar's Mate and I proudly stated, "Lots of times!" Jeffrey nodded and seemed to take some time considering my answer and then asked me, "The last time you won that way, what did you learn?" Actually—except for the fact that my opponent was vulnerable to this well-known trick—I hadn't learned a darned thing!

Jeffrey made me start to think of new opening ideas and encouraged me to learn a lot of new pawn formations. Until this time, I had never thought of pawn structures at all. Didn't pawns just get in the way? Or get wiped out? I'm as surprised today as I was then to learn how many chess openings there are—each with an unpronounceable name. Before delving into the enormous complexities of these openings, I'll share another principle I learned:

The underlying goal for all openings and defenses is to control the center.

This principle had not occurred to my earliest circle of chess friends. We happily traded pieces, pushed a pawn, delighted in a check, and hacked away at the opponent's army of chessmen. The idea that there should be an all-encompassing way of playing any opening was quite a surprise. The key squares are the four in the middle of the board: e4, d4, d5, and e5.

Diagram 14 shows the key central squares on the board, each marked with an X. The explanation for this principle is astonishingly simple: Put any piece on one of these squares, and it is at its most powerful. That's because the piece controls or influences more vital squares than if it's placed anywhere else. By controlling or occupying these squares, your pieces are more powerful than your opponent's—an advantage you can use to create attacks and win material!

Beyond the key central squares, a greater center covers sixteen squares (c3-c6-f6-f3), as shown in Diagram 15. By controlling this area of the board with pieces and pawns, a player is better able to conduct an attack on the Kingside or the Queenside flanks.

Armed with this understanding of the need to control the center, it became much easier for me to understand why some of the moves for

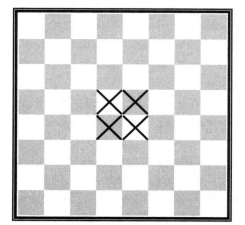

DIAGRAM 14.

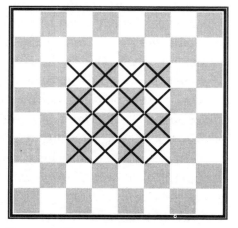

DIAGRAM 15.

those peculiar-sounding openings were played. It was at this point that game notation—writing down the moves of my games—became an important part of my development. I was able to analyze my games at home and learn if what I played was right or wrong. Along with writing down the moves to my own games, I now discovered that I could replay the games of other players. And some of these players were really good!

Early Opening Influences

The classic book, *Alexander Alekhine's Best Games*, by Alexander Alekhine (1982–1946, World Champion 1927–35, 1937–46), was inspiring to me. Alekhine had a turbulent style of play that I could not understand. His tactical flair was marvelous and he played a wide variety of openings and defenses. His play was beyond me, and his books helped me realize that I had a lot to learn.

America's Robert James (Bobby) Fischer (1943–, World Champion 1972–75) was another early influence. The 21 games played in his match against Boris Spassky (1937–, World Champion 1969–72) match brought endless hours of analysis with many players offering their suggestions and answering my questions. (If you use a computer program such as Chess Assistant or ChessBase, these games are probably in the database, which makes them easy to study.) During these analysis sessions I learned about the Sicilian Defense, Poisoned Pawn variation, the Queen's Gambit Declined (QGD), the Pirc Defense, and others. Bobby's favorite opening move was 1.e4 and it became mine too.

One further and important influence was a booklet called "The Max Lange Attack." The Max Lange Attack became my pet variation because of a pattern known as Legall's (Check) Mate.

Jeffrey enjoyed testing his young pupil and nearly every day he would set up a tactical quiz of some sort for me to solve. After setting up the pieces, he had me sit on the Black side. He would then let me ask questions about the game that he would select to be replayed. This aspect of chess thrilled me. We could replay any game that had been recorded *exactly* as it was first played. It was better than watching a movie because Jeffrey brought the play to life by indicating why a movement had been played. The following game is a classic, but sadly I have no idea who the players were.

Unknown Opponent versus Unknown Opponent

My Cannon and Queen Raid Openings had taken a back seat forever. I now fully appreciated the importance of developing the minor pieces as early as possible.

1.e4 e5   2.Nf3!

White develops a piece and attacks Black's e5-pawn.

2...d6

Black adopts a defense known as the *Philidor Defense*. Today's players consider the Philidor to be too passive, preferring instead to defend the e5-pawn with the classical 2...Nc6, or to counterattack White's e4-pawn with 2...Nf6, known as the *Petroff Defense*.

3.Bc4

White develops a piece while eyeing the f7-pawn. White's other major choice is 3.d4, attacking the e5-pawn and trying to gain a lead in development.

3...Bg4?!

Black is playing rather ambitiously by crossing into White's half of the board without the development necessary to back him up—not a particularly good idea. A better continuation is 3...Be7, intending to play ...Ng8-f6 and then castle kingside as soon as possible.

4.Nc3

White continues his development, but he has a number of more purposeful moves available. Any of the moves 4.h3, 4.d4, or 4.c3 lead to the establishment of a classical pawn center with d2-d4.

4...h6?

Black will be severely punished for this wasted move. Much better is 4...Nc6, which develops a piece and controls the e5 and d4 squares.

5.Nxe5!

This stunning move completely amazed me. This move puts White's Queen in jeopardy, which was all I needed to know to keep me from playing such a move. Without a second's hesitation, I showed my understanding of the position by capturing White's Queen, failing Jeffrey's quiz for that day.

5...Bxd1?

A bad error. Black should accept the loss of a pawn and play 5...dxe5 6.Qxg4 Nf6 7.Qg3 when White has won a pawn with advantage.

6.Bxf7+ Ke7   7.Nd5 Checkmate!

The final position, shown in Diagram 16, thrilled and delighted me. What a checkmate! Wow! Known as *Legall's Mate*, this mating pattern seemed to brand itself on my mind. I spent my next few games trying to repeat this same pattern on all my opponents! Unfortunately, no one ever gave me such an opportunity and so I was cast back to learning more about openings from Jeffrey.

Readers of the Microsoft Press chess series will recognize this game from *Play Winning Chess* (Microsoft Press, 1995). Repeating the pattern again emphasizes what an impact this sacrifice had on my chess development. White willingly lost his Queen—a whole Queen!—and pulled off a checkmate. Wow! Some beginners give up when they lose their Queen, the only piece they learned how to move.

DIAGRAM 16.

Introduction to Classical Openings

As soon as I began to compete with more experienced players, I had a new outlook: I really began to understand chess openings, the principles of play, pawn structures, controlling the center, protecting my King, open files, outposts, gambits, tactics, combinations—and even the names for most of them. Although the task of learning all this seemed Herculean at first, the opening principles are so clear that the moves just seemed to logically follow one another. This brings us to my next principle:

Strive to play stronger opponents.

Playing stronger opponents means losing lots of games and I certainly don't like losing! So to begin with, I shied away from opponents who would stomp on me with ease. On the other hand, I realized that I learned a lot more from my losses. Summoning up my courage, I began to play those who I knew would clobber me. The effort certainly paid off. Playing stronger opponents is simply the best way of improving your game. Studying is fine, but forging yourself in the fires of competition is the best.

The term *opening* refers to moves initiated by White (for example, "White opens the game with…"), and the term *defense* refers to Black's reaction. Classical openings fall into two separate groups:

- King Pawn openings, where White begins the game with 1.e4
- Queen Pawn openings, where White opens with 1.d4

Classical King Pawn openings and Queen Pawn openings, as well as their respective defenses, create different types of middle games. The nature of the play between the two groups of classical openings and defenses are very distinct. I can make some general comparisons:

King Pawn Openings	Queen Pawn Openings
Sharp play ensues immediately	The fight is delayed until later in the game
The King is more vulnerable	The King is less vulnerable
Calculating variations is fundamental	Strategic play is fundamental
An opening slip can cost the game	Opening slips aren't as meaningful
Certain lines require memorization	Memorizing lines is less necessary
The game is often shorter	The game usually lasts longer

As you can see, each of the two classical openings has different appealing aspects. If by nature you prefer to attack and you enjoy sharp forcing lines, then a King Pawn opening is a natural choice. If you prefer to build up your position by collecting small advantages, then a Queen Pawn opening is just your ticket. In the next two chapters, I take a deeper look at the Classics.

If, dear reader, you find these opening lines overwhelming, you're right! Panic! Chess openings are maddeningly complex. Mastering all the openings mentioned in this work requires years or even decades of study. My aim in this book is to point out these complexities and to offer you a solution. The solution will come later, as you must first understand the challenges faced!

CHAPTER THREE

Classical King Pawn Openings

You now understand that the key to getting a good position from the opening is to control the center—especially the four most central squares sometimes called "the sweet center"—with pawns and minor pieces. I'll now introduce a new concept: the idea of *equilibrium*. Take a fresh look at Diagram 17, the starting position. Both armies are perfect mirrors of one another. The opposing armies are in balance, or what Wilhelm Steinitz (1836–1900, World Champion 1886–94), the first officially recognized World Champion, called the equilibrium. Generations of chess players have debated the outcome of a game that was perfectly played by both sides. Would the games always be drawn? Because White *disturbs the equilibrium* by moving first, he gains the advantage of being able to develop

his army as well as to lay claim to a piece of the center. Black reacts in such a way as to *restore the equilibrium*. Thus there is a constant shifting in this elusive concept of the equilibrium. If White plays perfectly, then Black should always be playing catch up until the forces of both armies are exhausted (traded) and the game drawn. Theoretically then, a victory occurs when one side has made a mistake and the equilibrium can no longer be restored.

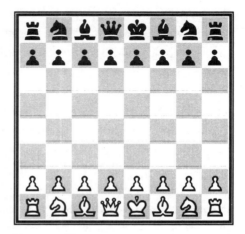

DIAGRAM 17.

Just because White moves first doesn't mean that he can only disturb the equilibrium in his favor. Can't White make a mistake? He certainly can. From the perspective of playing for control over the center, my Cannon Opening (1.h4) disturbs the equilibrium, but is a serious error! By my failing to play for control over the center, Black is given a free hand there and after 1...d5, Black has gained a central advantage and White's h4-pawn is a potential target.

After many generations of chess players have come and gone and with millions of games being played and recorded, we still resort to the most common opening moves:

1.e4

This opening move makes perfect sense. White's pawn occupies the e4-square and further controls the d5-square—the sweet center. White also opens up the diagonal for the f1-Bishop for quick development. White's Queen also has an avenue for possible development. However, you'll recall that one of the principles introduced in Chapter Two tells us to defer such a decision for now.

This opening move is called a *King Pawn Opening,* because the pawn directly in front of the King moves first.

Black now faces a dilemma. White's opening move has seized half of the sweet center. If allowed, White will seize the other half of the sweet center with 2.d4. Black's dilemma is how to combat White's opening move. What should be his approach to taking the center? The classical response is to match White's.

1...e5

The equilibrium is restored. Black's response has all the advantages of White's opening move, and now it is up to White to find a way to disturb the equilibrium in his favor.

What do you, dear reader, think of Black's move? Black's move should provoke your thoughts, and you might find it is a very worthwhile exercise to look at this move and ask a number of questions. What has Black accomplished by this move? What can White do? Black has taken a key foothold in the center; wouldn't it be wonderful to attack and remove the e5-pawn as soon as possible? Indeed it would. Virtually every move that attacks Black's e5-pawn and seeks its destruction has been tried and categorized! In chess openings, it seems that nothing is new under the sun.

White's most common and I believe best move is:

2.Nf3

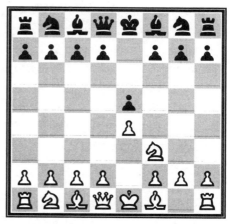

DIAGRAM 18.

As shown in Diagram 18, White develops a Knight, attacks the e5-pawn and covers the d4-square. White uses his move wisely, always with an eye toward controlling the sweet center and developing his forces.

Attacking the e5-pawn

Before I continue with the main line, consider a few of White's major options:

- ■ 2.Nc3, known as the *Vienna Game*
- ■ 2.Bc4, the *Bishop's Opening*
- ■ 2.c3, the *Center Pawn Opening*

Although these are viable options, the tries that I'll focus upon are those that seek to destroy the e5-pawn at once. The most consequent is:

2.d4

White immediately attacks the e5-pawn with his d4-pawn and seeks its removal. Black's choices are very limited. Defending the e5-pawn, in general, puts Black at a disadvantage.

| 2...d6?! | 3.dxe5! dxe5 |
| 4.Qxd8+ Kxd8 | |

In this resulting position, White has achieved a lot. Black has lost the opportunity to castle and his King has been forced to move.

5.Bc4

White attacks the f7-pawn, develops a piece, and has the superior game.

Now consider another line:

2.d4 Bd6?!

Black defends the e5-pawn, but the Bishop move allows White the opportunity to develop with tempo.

3.dxe5! Bxe5

4.Nf3

White attacks the Bishop. If the Bishop retreats by:

4...Bf6   5.e5! Be7

White has seized the advantage. Observe White's control over the sweet center. Furthermore, notice that White has developed two units of his army, his e5-pawn and f3-Knight, whereas Black has developed only one, his e7-Bishop.

6.Bc4!

White has developed his Kingside pieces and is prepared to play 7.O-O, thereby safely tucking away his King and allowing him to face the future with confidence.

Examine another approach to defending the e5-pawn:

2.d4 Nc6

This move defends the e5-pawn and counters with an attack against White's d4-pawn. This defense by Black is called the *Nimzovich Defense*. White has two choices. 3.d5 attacks Black's Knight and forces it to move again. The better alternative is:

3.dxe5 Nxe5

White succeeds in knocking Black's e5-pawn off the board, and in its place is a Knight that is vulnerable to attack. White can attack the e5-Knight with 4.Bf4, 4.f4, or:

4.Nf3 Nxf3+   5.Qxf3

White has eliminated Black's developed forces and has two units developed himself. White has gained the advantage.

Danish Gambit

The preceding lines show that when facing 2.d4, Black should not defend his e5-pawn on move two. Instead he should capture the d4-pawn:

    1.e4 e5   2.d4 exd4!

This is Black's best move. He wins a pawn and leaves it up to White to decide how to get it back.

    3.c3 dxc3   4.Nxc3

This is known as the *Danish Gambit*. White sacrifices a pawn but has developed two units, the e4-pawn and the c3-Knight. Black will have to catch up in development and comfort himself with the thought that he has won a pawn. The Danish Gambit is a particularly powerful gambit against beginning players.

Center Game

If White is not inclined to sacrifice a pawn he can try:

    1.e4 e5   2.d4 exd4!

    3.Qxd4

White has developed two units, whereas Black has developed none! On the surface this looks like a pretty good deal for White, except for one factor: White's Queen is vulnerable to attack and Black responds by developing his Knights.

    3...Nc6!

This move develops his Knight and forces White to move his Queen again. In this way, Black develops with tempo.

    4.Qe3 Nf6

Black has now caught up in development. This opening variation is called the *Center Game* and its main line continues:

    5.Nc3

While it seems like a good idea to attack Black's Knight with 5.e5, continuing with 5...Nd5 6.Qe4 Nb6 gives Black a fair game. Enterprising players might also like the gambit 5...Ng4 6.Qe2 d6! 7.exd6+ Be6 8.dxc7 Qxc7, in which Black sacrifices a pawn for a significant lead in development. We can conclude that 5.e5 would be premature.

    5...Bb4   **6.Bd2 O-O**
    7.O-O-O Re8!

This is the main line of the Center Game. Both sides have their trumps: White, with his e4-pawn, has more central influence with excellent attacking chances on the Kingside; Black has a ready-made attack on the e4-pawn with a possibility of further attacks upon White's Queen.

King's Gambit

As an alternative to attacking Black's e5-pawn with 2.d4, White has the centuries-old option of initiating the *King's Gambit*.

    1.e4 e5   **2.f4**

This line of play is fantastically complicated and dozens of books have been written on this popular gambit. Black can initiate *King's Gambit Accepted* by playing:

    2...exf4

White hopes to play Bc1xf4, thereby regaining the pawn with a superior position. White's position is considered superior because Black's e-pawn has moved twice (...e7-e5 and ...e5xf4), while White will have eliminated Black's e-pawn and developed a piece of his own. The two tempi that Black spent moving his pawn would be history.

    Black doesn't have to accept the gambit. He can play 2...Bc5 to initiate the *King's Gambit Classical Declined,* or he can try the *Falkbeer Counter Gambit* with 2...d5. Both variations have been greatly scrutinized by opening theorists who claim that Black gains a reasonable position with either move.

    3.Nf3

This develops a piece and blocks the possibility of ...Qd8-h4+, which would disturb White's King.

3...g5

Black shows his determination to hang onto his extra pawn. Black wants to rule out the possibility of Bc1xf4.

4.Bc4

White calmly develops his pieces and plays for the attack. A main alternative is 4.h4, which attempts to break up Black's Kingside.

4...g4

In a surprising move, Black also plays for the attack. By giving White's f3-Knight the boot, Black intends to play ...Qd8-h4+ the moment the f3-Knight moves.

5.O-O!?

White initiates the *Muzio Gambit* and willingly offers a Knight to increase his development. Playing 5.Ne5 Qh4+ 6.Kf1 Nf6 with the intention of playing ...Nf6-h5-g3+ can be dangerous for White. Such variations require careful study of the opening manuals.

5...gxf3

Black accepts the offered sacrifice.

6.Qxf3

White recaptures a pawn for the Knight, arriving at the position shown in Diagram 19.

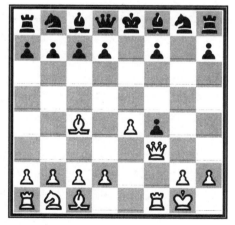

DIAGRAM 19.

The Muzio Gambit has been analyzed by generations of players. Does White have sufficient compensation for his Knight? The answer seems to be yes. Does he have enough compensation for the advantage? The answer is no. Most theorists consider the Muzio Gambit to be a draw. I encourage you to read other books to find out why!

Main Line, continued

To deal with White's crucial attempts to attack and obliterate the e5-pawn on move two, we've wandered a bit afield from the main line:

1.e4 e5   2.Nf3

Now reset the pieces and see the most common reaction:

2...Nc6

Black defends the e5-pawn and simultaneously guards the d4-square.

Petroff (or Russian) Defense

Even on move two, Black has another possible defensive move:

2...Nf6

This move initiates the *Petroff Defense*. (In Russia, it's called the *Russian Defense!*) Instead of busying himself with the defense of his e5-pawn, Black counters with an attack of his own against White's e4-pawn. The Petroff Defense, while considered a solid choice, is also considered a bit passive. White has two major options for attacking the e5-pawn once more: 3.Nxe5 or 3.d4. The choices are a matter of taste and study!

3.Nxe5 d6!   4.Nf3 Nxe4

Black has regained his pawn. White can muster a small advantage in a symmetrical position by:

5.Qe2 Qe7   6.d3 Nf6

7.Bg5 Qxe2+   8.Bxe2 Be7

White has a slight lead in development. Although this is not the best play for White, this line shows that White can ensure himself of a small opening advantage against the Petroff Defense.

Ruy Lopez (Main Line, continued)

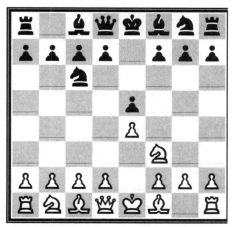

DIAGRAM 20.

Return once again to the main line:

1.e4 e5   2.Nf3 Nc6

These moves lead to the position shown in Diagram 20.

White now faces a major theoretical crossroad. The main line is:

3.Bb5

This move initiates the *Ruy Lopez Opening*. Most players simply call it "the Ruy." (Another common name for this line is the *Spanish Game*.)

The Ruy is arguably the oldest opening in chess. It can be traced to the sixteenth century, a time when the best players came from Spain. The opening is credited to Spanish priest Ruy Lopez (1530–80), who hailed from Estremadura, Spain.

The idea makes perfect sense. White wants to destroy the e5-pawn, which has one defender, the c6-Knight. So if White can capture the c6-Knight, the e5-pawn will likely wobble and fall.

Of course, White has other options for move three, which I describe in the following sections.

Scotch Game

Once again the most direct style of play is to attack the e5-pawn.

3.d4 exd4   4.Nxd4

The opening is called the *Scotch Game.* Today's highest-rated player, Garry Kasparov (1963–, World Champion 1985–present), has employed the Scotch Game from time to time with enormous success. Black gains nothing from trading Knights by 4...Nxd4? 5.Qxd4. White's Queen—although prematurely developed—is hardly assailable in the middle of the board in this position. Black's best play is thought to be an attack on the e4-pawn:

4...Nf6   5.Nxc6

White feels obligated to make this trade. After 5.Nc3 Bb4, the e4-pawn comes under attack yet again.

5...bxc6   6.e5

White makes the most of his e4-pawn. After 6.Bd3 d5 7.exd5 cxd5 the game is considered dynamically balanced.

6...Qe7

Black resumes the attack on White's e-pawn yet again.

7.Qe2 Nd5

At last, Black's Knight is forced to give way. While White has accomplished his goal of obliterating Black's e5-pawn, the position isn't all that rosy for him. Black stands but one move away from neutralizing the position with ...d7-d6, which knocks out White's e5-pawn.

8.c4

White now seeks to boot the d5-Knight to a passive square.

8...Ba6

DIAGRAM 21.

Black pins White's c4-pawn to the Queen and brings about the position shown in Diagram 21.

This position from the Scotch Game is one of the most awkward positions for either side to play. Once more, I encourage further study of this position from manuals devoted to this fascinating opening.

Italian Game

When I began my career, my favorite opening variation was:

1.e4 e5   2.Nf3 Nc6
3.Bc4

These moves initiate the *Italian Game*. Diagram 22 shows the starting position of the Italian Game. Besides the sound idea of developing a piece and preparing to castle Kingside, the thematic idea behind the Italian Game is to take clear aim at the f7-pawn and, by extension, Black's King. The Italian Game is a dangerous opening for Black and he has to navigate some tricky tactical lines.

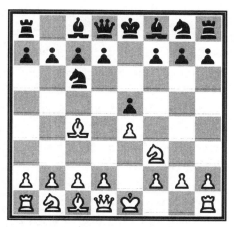

DIAGRAM 22.

3...Bc5

This is a reasonable move, as Black also develops his Bishop.

Two Knights Defense and Traxler Gambit

A key alternative for Black following 1.e4 e5 2.Nf3 Nc6 3.Bc4 is:

3...Nf6

Black counters with an attack against the e4-pawn, initiating the *Two Knights Defense*. White can shore up his e4-pawn by 4.d3 or 4.Nc3, or he can initiate a complex attack:

4.Ng5

This attacking move has been debated for centuries! By continuing to attack the f7-pawn, White plays consistently. But with only two pieces developed, is White's attack premature? In my younger days, attacking was the most enjoyable aspect of chess and I certainly didn't hesitate making this move. Nowadays I'm no longer sure the attack is correct. It seems that the f7-pawn can't be defended, but the attack can be blocked:

4...d5

As always there is a key alternative. Black can sacrifice the f7-pawn in a gambit! 4...Bc5, called the *Traxler Gambit*, offers the f7-pawn. White should play 5.Bxf7+, because the natural 5.Nxf7 Bxf2+! 6.Kxf2 Nxe4+ 7.Kg1 Qh4 8.g3 Nxg3! has been worked out to a draw. Therefore (1.e4 e5 2.Nf3 Nc6 3.Bc4 Nf6 4.Ng5 Bc5) 5.Bxf7+ Ke7 6.Bd5 is the often-played line for White. Black has lost a pawn and compromised his King. By continuing 6...Rf8 7.Nf3 d6 8.d3 Bg4, Black has ample development for his lost pawn. As always, I encourage further study of the pertinent opening manuals.

5.exd5

Diagram 23 shows the resulting position, the main position of the Two Knights Defense.

Black has a number of ways to play the position, all of which have been scrutinized at great length. One alternative is 5...Na5 6.Bb5+ c6 7.dxc6 bxc6 8.Be2 h6 9.Nf3. White's pieces have been beaten backwards, but Black has lost a pawn. Play most often continues 9...e4 10.Ne5 Qd4 11.f4 Bc5 12.Rf1, with a complex game ahead as both players have their trumps.

Another major choice from Diagram 23 is 5...b5, the *Ulvestad Varia-tion*, a surprising move that aims to deflect White's Bishop away from the f7-pawn. Continuing: 6.Bxb5 Qxd5 7.Nc3 Qxg2 8.Qf3 Qxf3 9.Nxf3 Bd7 10.O-O Bd6 11.Bxc6 Bxc6 12.Nxe5 Bxe5 13.Re1. This line is considered slightly advantageous for White.

DIAGRAM 23.

Fried Liver Attack

Return to Diagram 23 and play the main line. To recap:

1.e4 e5	**2.Nf3 Nc6**
3.Bc4 Nf6	**4.Ng5 d5**
5.exd5 Nxd5	

Black has sensibly recaptured the pawn and is now eyeballing White's g5-Knight. Not to be deterred, White boldly plunges ahead:

6.Nxf7 Kxf7   7.Qf3+

With this move, White initiates the colorfully named *Fried Liver Attack*. White has a double attack against King and the d5-Knight, forcing Black's King into the center.

7...Ke6

By placing his monarch in the midst of the battle, Black hangs onto the extra Knight at a dangerous price. White continues to attack the d5-Knight, which is a feint. Black's King soon becomes a target as well!

8.Nc3 Nce7   9.d4!

White makes an excellent move in an attempt to pry open the center.

9...c6!

It would be a mistake to play 9...exd4 10.Nxd5 Nxd5 11.Qe4+!, whereby White regains his sacrificed Knight.

Diagram 24 shows the current position, where Black has defended the Knight once more. Playing the Fried Liver Attack as White brought me hours of joy. I'd do my best to bring my pieces into play as quickly as possible, while Black would try to hang onto his extra piece and to bring his King back to the relatively safe c7-square. Diagram 24 deserves close study, and I recommend playing the position out with your friends to determine which side has best disturbed the equilibrium!

Evans Gambit

Return now to Diagram 22 and the Italian Game, which starts 1.e4 e5 2.Nf3 Nc6 3.Bc4. Continue with:

3...Bc5

From this position, White has four main options:

■ 4.O-O

DIAGRAM 24.

■ 4.b4!? (Evans Gambit)

■ 4.c3 (Giuoco Piano)

■ 4.d4!? (Max Lange Attack)

I'll discuss each option in turn.

The first option, 4.O-O, brings his King to safety, which is quite reasonable, but the move isn't considered that dynamic. Black plays 4...Nf6, continuing a balanced game.

4.b4!?

This energetic pawn sacrifice is known as the *Evans Gambit*. As usual, the idea behind the gambit is to pick up a lead in development. Black must accept the gambit:

4...Bxb4   5.c3

White attacks the Bishop in order to support the central thrust, d2-d4.

5...Ba5   6.d4

White reveals his strategy. He wants to open up the center, anticipating that his development will bring him the superior game.

6...exd4

Some theorists prefer 6...d6! 7.Qb3 Qd7 as the correct defensive continuation.

7.O-O dxc3

Black greedily captures all the morsels being offered. Diagram 25 shows the current position.

Black has captured three pawns, but his position is dangerously behind in development. White quickly goes on the offensive:

8.Qb3! Qf6   9.e5!

With a move that is even stronger than 9.Bg5, White also gains a tempo. Black's Queen must now guard the f7-pawn:

9...Qg6   10.Nxc3 Nge7

11.Ba3! O-O   12.Rad1

White's development is a thing of beauty. His pieces are poised for central domination and Black's position is under a great deal of pressure. The two pawns are a heavy investment, but Black will almost certainly have to give back his material gains to neutralize White's pressure. This is another position with which you should challenge your friends, playing alternating sides.

DIAGRAM 25.

Giuoco Piano

Another option for White's move four in the Italian Game, which starts 1.e4 e5 2.Nf3 Nc6 3.Bc4 Bc5, is:

4.c3

This is quite a direct attempt by White to grab the center. Just as in the Evans Gambit, White insists on playing d2-d4, which attacks the e5-pawn and, as an added bonus, the c5-Bishop. This move is known as the *Giuoco Piano*. Black is quick to respond in the center too:

4...Nf6   5.d4

White continues to play in the center.

5...exd4   6.cxd4

The position in Diagram 26 makes a very agreeable impression. White's two central e4- and d4-pawns create a formation called the *classical pawn center*. It seems that White has achieved all that he could hope for and best of all, with tempo! Furthermore, Black's c5-Bishop is attacked. But before dismissing Diagram 26 as superior for White, let me ask

DIAGRAM 26.

you a question: Has Black made a mistake? I can't see how Black's previous moves were wrong. Therefore, if Black hasn't made a mistake, has the equilibrium been disturbed to his disadvantage? The answer can only be no! It is these very fundamental, basic questions which will help you in your quest for opening understanding. By constantly asking such questions, you will help yourself find the truth in your favorite openings. How should Black continue?

6...Bb4+   7.Bd2

White blocks the check. White could try 7.Nc3 Nxe4 8.O-O Bxc3 9.d5, initiating the *Moeller Attack.* Theorists consider this line to be all bark and no bite. By continuing 9...Bf6 10.Re1 Ne7 11.Rxe4 d6, Black has a fine game.

7...Bxd2+   8.Nbxd2 d5!

In a crucial reaction, White's classic center is destroyed.

9.exd5 Nxd5   10.Qb3 Nce7

Diagram 27 shows the main position of the Giuoco Piano, which practice has shown to be roughly equal.

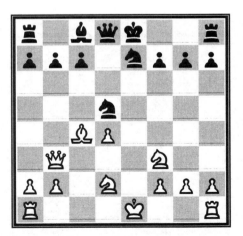

DIAGRAM 27.

Max Lange Attack

My favorite choice for move four in the Italian Game (1.e4 e5 2.Nf3 Nc6 3.Bc4 Bc5) is:

4.d4!?

This move starts the *Max Lange Attack.* I enjoy making this paradoxical sacrifice. Black has geared his development toward controlling the d4-square and undeterred, White places a pawn squarely in Black's jaws. This startling move makes a lot of sense in the Italian Game. With the Evans Gambit and

Giuoco Piano, White aims for d2-d4 with a preparatory move, spending a tempo. My attitude: Why waste a move? Black gleefully accepts the offering:

4...exd4

This is the main line of the Max Lange. A key alternative is 4...Bxd4 5.Bg5 Nf6 (5...f6 6.Nxd4 Nxd4 7.Be3 Ne6 8.O-O completes White's development and gives him a chance to attack with Qd1-h5+) 6.Nxd4 Nxd4 7.f4 d6 8.f5, in which White has sacrificed a pawn for an annoying bind. My opponents usually preferred the main line:

5.O-O Nf6

Once more, Black can avoid the main line by 5...d6 6.c3 dxc3 7.Nxc3, when White has shed a pawn for a dangerous lead in development.

6.e5 d5!

In many variations of the classical King Pawn openings, this rejoinder is a key counterpunch. If Black is forced to move his f6-Knight, disaster strikes quickly: 6...Ng4? 7.Bxf7+ Kxf7 8.Ng5+ Kg8 9.Qxg4 Nxe5 10.Qe4 d6 11.Qd5+ Kf8 12.f4!, when White wins.

7.exf6 dxc4   8.Re1+ Be6

9.Ng5

This was my early favorite line of opening play. What a joy it was to play this position (shown in Diagram 28) as White! Black has but one saving move:

9...Qd5!

I enjoyed a number of victories after the weaker 9...Qxf6? 10.Nxe6 fxe6 11.Qh5+ g6 12.Qxc5! spears a Bishop. Another bad mistake is 9...O-O? 10.fxg7 Kxg7 (10...Re8 11.Qh5 Bf5?? 12.Qxf7 Checkmate!) 11.Rxe6! White wins a Bishop with a

DIAGRAM 28.

raging attack, and Black can't regain the lost piece by 11...h6? 12.Rxh6! because White's Rook seems to enjoy a charmed life. Every time Black tries to capture the invading Rook, he loses his Queen.

From Diagram 28, the Max Lange Attack continues:

10.Nc3!

A wonderful move! I derive pleasure from moves where I place my pieces in capture, but they can't be taken. This is life on the edge! In this position, it is a good move; White develops with a gain of tempo.

10...Qf5

The Queen has to move. The Knight is quite safe: 10...dxc3?? 11.Qxd5 wins the Queen.

11.Nce4 O-O-O

Black escapes the center and the Kingside while he has the chance. Capturing the f6-pawn by 11...gxf6? 12.g4! Qe5 (keeping the c5-Bishop protected) 13.f4! d3+ 14.Kf1 Qd4 15.Be3 is excellent for White.

12.g4! Qe5   13.fxg7 Rhg8
14.Nxe6 fxe6   15.Bh6

The current position is shown in Diagram 29.

DIAGRAM 29.

I enjoy playing this main line Max Lange Attack position, scoring heavily with the White pieces. From this line, you should have gained an appreciation for the complexity of this classical opening variation. Yet it isn't even the main variation! I've led us far astray.

Alternatives to the Ruy Lopez Main Line

Return with me to Diagram 20 (1.e4 e5 2.Nf3 Nc6). From this position,

3.Bb5 initiates the Ruy Lopez Opening. It has long been held that White's third move puts the most pressure on Black's position. There is the constant threat of White's capturing the c6-Knight and snipping the e5-pawn. Black's earliest defenses include:

- ■ 3...d6 (Steinitz Defense)
- ■ 3...Nge7 (Cozio Defense)
- ■ 3...Nf6 (Berlin Defense)
- ■ 3...Nd4 (Bird Defense)
- ■ 3...Bc5 (Classical Defense)
- ■ 3...f5 (Schliemann Defense)

Steinitz Defense

Making a sensible decision, Black reinforces his e5-pawn.

3...d6

Nowadays this move, called the *Steinitz Defense,* is considered too passive. Black locks in his f8-Bishop and gives White a free hand in the center:

4.d4! exd4   5.Nxd4 Bd7

The effects of the opening moves have favored White. He has better control of the center and freer piece play. Many games continue thus:

6.O-O Nf6   7.Nc3 Be7
8.Re1 O-O

Practice has shown that White has the advantage.

Cozio Defense

Black covers his c6-Knight but also compromises his f8-Bishop in a line called the *Cozio Defense,* which is favored by few players today.

3...Nge7   4.O-O d6
5.d4 Bd7

Black reveals his point. He hasn't been forced to trade his strong e5-pawn.

6.Re1 Ng6

Black continues to keep his e5-pawn protected. In return, however, White now gains a d5-outpost:

7.Nc3! Be7   8.Nd5 O-O

Black has a safe, if passive, game.

Berlin Defense

Not concerning himself with the e5-pawn, Black attacks White's e4-pawn as in the Petroff Defense.

3...Nf6

This move initiates the *Berlin Defense,* which continues to be popular even in modern chess tournaments. Theoretically, White should avoid playing 4.d3 Bc5! because he will need to utilize the strike d2-d4 to prove an advantage.

4.O-O

White leaves the e4-pawn en prise, reasoning that he will soon win the pawn back.

4...Nxe4   5.d4!

This is White's point. With Black's King still in the center, White wants to rip open the e-file. The Berlin Defense continues:

5...Nd6

It would be unwise to play 5...exd4? 6.Re1 d5 7.Nxd4, leaving White with the dangerous threats of Nd4xc6 and f2-f3.

6.Bxc6 bxc6

The Berlin also offers the intriguing ending 6...dxc6 7.dxe5 Nf5 8.Qxd8+ Kxd8, which at first glance seems bad for Black. This line was championed by Emanuel Lasker (1868–1941, World Champion 1894–1921), the second official World Champion, who felt that Black's two Bishops were sufficient compensation for losing the right to castle and the doubled Queenside pawns.

7.dxe5 Nb7   8.Re1 Be7
9.Nc3 O-O   10.Qe2 Nc5

Diagram 30 shows the main position of the Berlin Defense. Theory considers the position slightly better for White.

Bird Defense

A second leap of the Knight, called the *Bird Defense,* represents a radical solution by Black.

3...Nd4(?!)

He moves the same developed piece twice, which gives me a chance to introduce another principle:

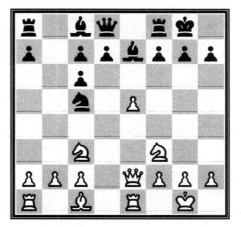

DIAGRAM 30.

Whenever possible, avoid moving the same piece twice in the opening.

This principle should serve as a guide and a warning. It is not to be taken as a rule! If a piece is attacked and is forced to move, then by all means do so! The principle is that players should develop all their forces as quickly as possible. By singling out just one piece, a player is neglecting the rest of the crowd.

The purpose of the Bird Defense is to get away from White's Bishop and to control the d4-square. Play continues:

4.Nxd4! exd4   5.O-O c6

6.Ba4

White moves his developed Bishop twice—violating my latest principle—but is forced to do so. The Bishop is attacked.

6...Nf6   7.d3 d5

8.Bg5 dxe4

Weaker is 8...Be7 9.Bxf6 Bxf6 10.exd5 Qxd5 11.Re1+ Be6?! 12.Bb3, which gives the advantage to White.

9.dxe4 Be7   10.e5 Nd5

11.Bxe7 Nxe7   12.Bb3 O-O

13.Nd2

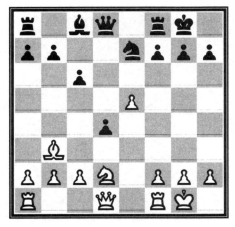

DIAGRAM 31.

Diagram 31 shows the result of the Bird Defense, which theorists consider advantageous for White.

Classical Defense
Another response to the Ruy Lopez Opening is the *Classical Defense*.

3...Bc5

Black ignores White's play and instead develops his own Bishop. This reasonable decision asks White how he intends to further his central influence.

4.c3

As we've seen, White prepares to establish a classical pawn center with d2-d4.

4...Nf6

Unimpressed, Black responds with a counterattack to the e4-pawn. This line is quite comparable with the Giuoco Piano variation (Diagram 26); the key difference is that White's Bishop is on the b5-square instead of the c4-square. This difference means that the sting of a possible ...d7-d5 counter will be missing.

5.d4 exd4 6.e5!

Now Black's f6-Knight is forced to move. The counter 6...d5? 7.exf6 would cost Black a piece.

6...Ne4 7.O-O!

White exploits a crucial nuance. Black's forces in the center are awkward. Black had expected 7.cxd4 Bb4+ 8.Bd2 Nxd2 9.Nbxd2 O-O 11.a3 Bxd2 12.Qxd2 d6 with a balanced game.

7...d5

Capturing by 7...dxc3? 8.Qd5! c2 9.Qxe4 cxb1=Q (this is a busy pawn!) 10.Rxb1 gives White a grand lead in development for the price of a pawn.

8.Nxd4!

This move is even stronger than 8.cxd4 Bb6 9.Nc3, which is also favorable for White.

8...O-O

Diagram 32 shows the current position.

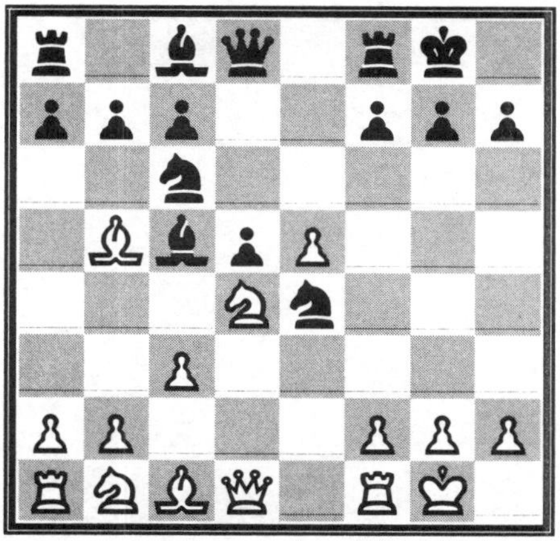

9.Bxc6!

White avoids 9.Nxc6 bxc6 10.Bxc6 Ba6!, rightfully concerned that the coordinated attack on the f2-pawn would be good for Black.

DIAGRAM 32.

9...bxc6   10.f3!

This is stronger than 10.Nxc6 Qh4, where Black again attacks the f2-pawn.

10...Ng5   11.Be3 Ne6
12.f4

White has the advantage.

Schliemann Defense

The *Schliemann Defense* is a plain old ornery reaction to the Ruy. Black reasons that since White's Bishop isn't patrolling the a2-g8 diagonal, he can counterattack White's center with this dangerous pawn thrust.

3...f5!?

Black takes a risk by loosening up the defenses around his King, but White has to be careful to prove an opening advantage:

4.Nc3

The cautious 4.d3 fxe4 5.dxe4 Nf6 6.O-O d6 7.Qd3 Be7 8.Qc4 is slightly better for White because Black has weakened himself on the a2-g8 diagonal.

4...fxe4   5.Nxe4 d5

Black goes all out for the fight for the initiative. White can no longer play cautiously and must ride the tiger.

DIAGRAM 33.

6.Nxe5 dxe4 7.Nxc6 Qd5!

This leads to Diagram 33, which is a mess. Theorists have wrestled with this position for some time. White should continue:

8.c4 Qd6 9.Qh5+ g6
10.Qe5+ Qxe5 11.Nxe5+ c6
12.Ba4

There is an important trick worth memorizing: After 12.Nxc6? a6! 13.Ba4 Bd7!, Black snares a piece.

12...Bg7 13.d4 exd3
14.Bf4

These moves provide a sharp game that isn't unfavorable for Black. The Schliemann Defense remains one of the sharpest adventures in the Ruy. Players be warned! This variation requires careful preparation!

Morphy's Defense (Main Line, continued)

Return now to the Ruy Lopez main line (1.e4 e5 2.Nf3 Nc6 3.Bb5).

3...a6!

This move, introduced by Paul Morphy (1837–84), puts the question to White's Bishop of its intentions. It is based upon the tactical resource 4.Bxc6 dxc6 5.Nxe5 Qd4!, when Black recaptures the e-pawn under favorable circumstances. *Morphy's Defense* has become the favored move for a century.

White is faced with a choice: Should he trade his Bishop for a Knight, or should the Bishop retreat?

Ruy Lopez Exchange Variation

The Ruy Lopez *Exchange Variation* has had entire books devoted to it.

4.Bxc6 dxc6

Diagram 34 shows quite an enigma. Which player profits best from the trade? Most grandmasters prefer Bishops to Knights, but no less a player than Bobby Fischer liked to trot out the Exchange Variation on occasion. White has a long-term endgame advantage due to the doubled pawns, but Black has a middle game with two Bishops before him.

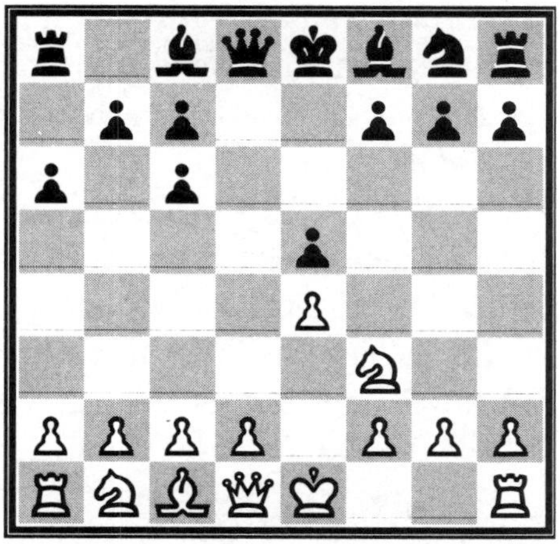

Standard play continues:

5.O-O

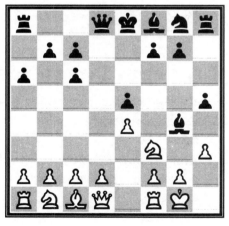

DIAGRAM 34.

5.Nxe5 Qd4 6.Nf3 Qxe4+ 7.Qe2 Qxe2+ 8.Kxe2 Bg4 is a comfortable variation for the second player.

5...Bg4!

Black puts his Bishop to work immediately. Another favored choice is 5...f6 6.d4 Bg4 7.dxe5 Qxd1 8.Rxd1 fxe5 9.Rd3 Bd6, with approximately equal play.

6.h3

White borrows a page from Black's opening book by questioning the Bishop's intentions.

6...h5!

A snappy retort! Black wants to keep the pin as long as he can. White has a small plus after 6...Bxf3 7.Qxf3 Qd7 because Black's pawn structure has been compromised. Worse, 6...Bh5? 7.g4 Bg6 8.Nxe5 Bxe4? 9.Re1 will be disastrous for Black.

Diagram 35 shows the current position. White has to navigate his

DIAGRAM 35.

way to an advantage with care. It is easy to go wrong. As you might guess, capturing Black's Bishop is a direct path to disaster. (Take heart, I took the Bishop and lost the first time I reached this position.) Best is:

7.d3!

Capturing the Bishop opens up the h-file to a checkmating attack: 7.hxg4? hxg4 8.Nxe5? Qh4! 9.f4 g3 and White can resign with confidence. There are no hidden brilliant moves to stave off checkmate. Nor can White pull off a central buildup like in the Italian game: 7.c3 Qd3! Black threatens to capture White's Knight and double up White's pawns. Continuing: 8.hxg4 hxg4 9.Nxe5 Bd6! 10.Nxd3 Bh2+ 11.Kh1 Bd6+ ends in a draw by perpetual check.

7...Qf6

This early development of the Queen is correct in this position. As we've seen, Black aims to double White's pawns.

8.Be3

White develops his pieces and acquiesces to doubled pawns. He could have tried 8.Nbd2, preventing Black from completing his threat, but his development is thereby blocked. Black would continue with 8...Ne7 menacing ...Ne7-g6-f4. Once more, continuing 9.hxg4? hxg4 10.Nh2? Qh4 works splendidly for Black.

8...Bxf3   9.Qxf3 Qxf3

10.gxf3 Bd6

The position is considered equal.

Ruy Lopez (Main Line, continued)

Because the Exchange Variation results in an approximately equal position, White's Bishop usually retreats (1.e4 e5 2.Nf3 Nc6 3.Bb5 a6):

4.Ba4

Diagram 36 shows the current position of the main line.

White retains his Bishop and keeps up the pressure on the a4-e8 diagonal.

4...Nf6

Black happily brings his Knight into battle, confronting White with the issue of what he wants to do about his e4-pawn. If he was so inclined, Black could play 4...b5 5.Bb3, with play similar to the Italian Game. Playing 3.Bb5 a6 4.Ba4 b5 5.Bb3 is favorable for White when compared to 3.Bc4 for several reasons. On the b3-square, White's Bishop is less vulnerable than on the c4-square— especially when Black tries varia- tions with the ...d7-d5 shot. Fur-

DIAGRAM 36.

thermore, the b5-pawn is a potential weakness. White might play a2-a4 to expose such a weakness.

5.O-O

Countless games have proven that only this move offers White a chance for an advantage. Defending the e4-pawn by 5.Nc3 Bc5 6.d3 d6 is a harm- less line. Equally timid is 5.d3 Bc5 6.c3 b5 7.Bc2 d5, when Black has good play. White's final defensive try is 5.Qe2 b5 6.Bb3 Be7 7.a4 Rb8 8.axb5 axb5, with equal play.

The current position, shown in Diagram 37, brings Black to a major crossroad. He has to choose between the Ruy Lopez *Open Varia- tion* with 5...Nxe4, or the Ruy Lopez *Closed Variation* with 5...Be7.

The Closed Variation is the deci- sion preferred by most grandmas- ters and constitutes the main line.

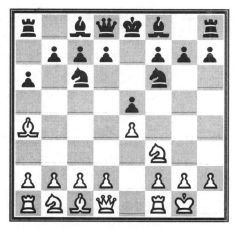

DIAGRAM 37.

Ruy Lopez Open Variation

How does the Open Ruy work?

5...Nxe4   6.d4!

White seeks to open the position to his advantage by forcing pawn trades. Keep in mind that White's King is nice and safe whereas Black's King is several tempi away from vacating the center. Opening the position potentially endangers Black's monarch.

6...b5

It would be a mistake to play 6...exd4? 7.Re1 d5 8.Bg5, as Black would be in a precarious situation.

7.Bb3 d5!

Black reins in his ambitions of winning pawns. Black avoids 7...exd4? 8.Re1 d5 9.Nc3! Be6 (9...dxc3 10.Bxd5 Bb7 11.Bxe4 Be7 12.Qe2 freezes Black's King in the center) 10.Nxe4 dxe4 11.Rxe4 Be7 12.Bxe6 fxe6 13.Nxd4! because White would recover his pawns with advantage.

8.dxe5 Be6

This leads to the key starting position of the Open Ruy, shown in Diagram 38.

The position is extremely dynamic and hard to judge. Black's Queenside is extended and vulnerable to a possible a2-a4. The d5-pawn is also a possible target but this isn't usually Black's Achilles' heel. Black's advanced d- and b-pawns have left the c5-square lacking protection and as play unfolds, White tries to conquer this square. On the plus side, White's e5-pawn isn't having a disruptive impact. Black's pieces are all potent and he has every expectation of a fighting game. White's three major tries are 9.Qe2, 9.c3, and 9.Nbd2. A number of these variations have transposi-

DIAGRAM 38.

tions. All three lines are extremely complex and books have been devoted to them! My recommendation for White is to play the forcing:

9.Nbd2

Threatening to capture on e4, White disrupts Black's position. The benefit of this move is that it forces play into a narrow line.

    9...Nc5   **10.c3**

White makes room to retreat his b3-Bishop.

    10...d4

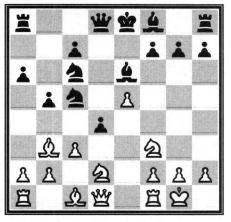

DIAGRAM 39.

Practice shows that this move is required. White gets a favorable bind following 10...Nxb3 11.Nxb3 Be7 12.Nfd4! Nxd4 13.cxd4, and he has control over the c5-square.

    Diagram 39, after Black's tenth move, shows the key position of the Open Ruy Lopez.

    11.Ng5!

Practice has shown that this incredible move makes life difficult for Black. The tactical justification for this move is that 11...Qxg5?! 12.Qf3 Kd7 13.Bd5! is good for White. I encourage you to do further research on this exciting and dynamic position.

Ruy Lopez Closed Variation
(Main Line, continued)

In the meantime, return to the main line (1.e4 e5 2.Nf3 Nc6 3.Bb5 a6 4.Ba4 Nf6 5.O-O):

    5...Be7

This initiates the Ruy Lopez Closed Variation. Black quite contentedly develops his Bishop and prepares to exit his King to safety. White again is asked to find a way of disturbing the equilibrium to his favor. The path is rather narrow.

Delayed Exchange Ruy Lopez

White has two key choices. He can play the main line, 6.Re1, defending the e4-pawn. Or he can play the *Delayed Exchange Ruy Lopez:*

6.Bxc6

Besides these two main variations, White can play 6.d3, simply shoring up the e4-pawn and planning to complete his development. This, however, is the move that Black has been waiting for. Black so far has avoided ...d7-d6, fearing the immediate reaction d2-d4. Once White has played 6.d3 d6!, Black doesn't have to worry about d2-d4 and the pressure on his position is quite tolerable.

The stutter step by White's Bishop, Bb5-a4xc6, seems to lose time.

6...dxc6

Isn't Black better off than in the usual Ruy Lopez Exchange Variation? Yes and no. White reasons that the extra moves presented to Black have prevented him from utilizing defenses based upon ...Bc8-g4 or ...f7-f6 and that the e5-pawn is under more pressure than before.

7.Re1

After this move, Black is in a bit of a quandary. How will he defend his e5-pawn? Both 7...Bd6 or 7...Qd6 are met by 8.d4, whereupon 8...exd4? 9.e5 will cost Black material. Neither does 7...Bg4 8.h3 suffice. Black can't play 8...h5? 9.hxg4 hxg4 10.Nxe5, as White wins a piece. In this case, Black no longer has an attack down the h-file. Thus the Delayed Exchange Ruy Lopez has its fans. Black's best move is:

7...Nd7   8.d4 exd4

9.Nxd4 Nc5

Diagram 40 shows the current position.

White has given up the two Bishops for a structural advantage. The position is approximately equal and is another good position to play against a friend.

Ruy Lopez Closed Variation (Main Line, continued)

Most grandmasters prefer not to give up their a4-Bishop at move six and instead continue (1.e4 e5 2.Nf3 Nc6 3.Bb5 a6 4.Ba4 Nf6 5.O-O Be7):

6.Re1

This move reinforces the e4-pawn and renews the threat of Ba4xc6 and Nf3xe5, as shown in Diagram 41. While this sixth move of White

DIAGRAM 40.

is the most common choice and indeed the main line, it also is a violation of my latest principle! White moves the same piece, his Rook, twice. Isn't this move a waste of time?

This is one of the great chess debates. When a player castles, he moves both King and Rook at the same time, the only moment when moving two pieces at once is allowed. Many centuries ago, the movement of castling was considered so valuable, the player was charged with *two* moves. A player would first move his King and then after his opponent had moved, he would then be obliged to move his Rook. Castling is a wonderful privilege that should be coveted. The King sprints to a flank and is usually out of harm's way. The Rook is developed and put into action. The rules of chess classify castling as a movement of the

DIAGRAM 41.

63

King. Thus, players would argue that White doesn't waste a tempo by moving his Rook to the center.

I urge you to review the principles listed in Chapter Two in order to form an opinion about this move. Although the move is classified as a King move, I believe that when castling the Rook is also developed. After castling, I much prefer to leave the Rook right on the square where it lands *unless I'm obligated to do otherwise.*

In Diagram 41, White's Rook reinforces control over the sweet center. More importantly, however, White didn't have a convenient way of defending his e4-pawn. As we've seen, White is trying to create a classical pawn center by playing for both e4- and d4-pawns to stand abreast of one another. If White plays 6.d3, then Black responds 6...d6 and has nothing to fear. Similarly, 6.Nc3 b5 7.Bb3 isn't so useful. Black plays 7...O-O and asks White if 8.d4 is his intention.

Quiz. Can you figure out what Black would do after 1.e4 e5 2.Nf3 Nc6 3.Bb5 a6 4.Ba4 Nf6 5.O-O Be7 6.Nc3 b5 7.Bb3 O-O 8.d4? The solution is at the end of this chapter.

This brings me to another opening principle:
To be effective, Rooks belong on open files. When there are no open files, centralize your Rooks to the e- and d-files.

On the e-file, White's Rook provides potent backup to the e4-pawn. If Black tries to play ...d7-d5 and knock the e4-pawn out of the way, White's Rook will then be open for operations down the e-file.

White's 6.Re1 restores the lingering threat to capture the c6-Knight and then the e5-pawn. Black addresses this threat with a tempo by:

6...b5   7.Bb3

White moves his Bishop for a third time in the space of seven moves! Is this not terrible? Well, yes it is. White has spent a lot of moves upon his Bishop, but he didn't *waste* these moves. He moved his Bishop when it was attacked by Black's pawns. While Black has *developed* his pawns with tempo, their advances can also be argued as a potential *weakness*. The squares that these pawns once controlled have to find other means of protection. Black now moves his King to safety:

7...O-O

This move brings us to the position pictured in Diagram 42, a position that has likely been seen more often than any other opening. The play of

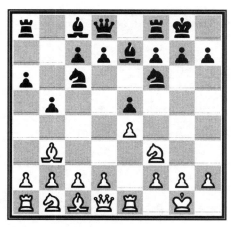

DIAGRAM 42.

both sides has been sensible and straightforward. Both players have been developing their forces and protecting their Kings, all while playing for central control. Which side stands better? This question really has no answer, for the game is still beginning! From this position, reams of analysis and opening ideas have been catalogued.

White has three main moves: 8.a4, 8.d4, and the main line, 8.c3.

Ruy Lopez Anti-Marshall Variation

The Ruy Lopez *Anti-Marshall Variation* offers a bit of a surprise and a marked departure from the usual focus upon the sweet center.

8.a4

This move aims to prove that Black's b-pawn sticks out like a sore thumb and deserves a little attention. White's obvious threat of 9.axb5 provokes a response:

8...Bb7

Black protects his a8-Rook and eyes the e4-pawn.

9.d3

At long last, White commits his d-pawn.

9...d6

65

DIAGRAM 43.

And Black does the same. With the e5-pawn now firmly protected, the question of an advantage is decided by which player will best activate his pieces.

10.Nc3

White develops with tempo, and the b5-pawn is still a target.

10...b4   11.Ne2

Seeking to reposition the Knight on the Kingside, White has fewer possibilities for an advantage after 11.Nd5?! Nxd5 12.Bxd5 Na5!

11...Na5   12.Ba2 c5
13.Ng3

In this position, shown in Diagram 43, White is considered to have a small advantage due to a likely Kingside attack. Certainly, chess books are filled with games played from this position. Still, most grandmasters prefer to play the main line.

One other interesting try is going after the center:

8.d4

This move involves a sacrifice:

8...Nxd4!   9.Nxd4

White has to sidestep 9.Nxe5?! Nxb3 10.axb3 Bb7 due to Black's powerful Bishops.

9...exd4   10.e5

White must avoid 10.Qxd4? c5! 11.Qd1 c4, which snares the b3-Bishop.

10...Ne8   11.c3! dxc3
12.Nxc3

White has sacrificed a pawn for superior development. Theorists don't consider this gambit to be good enough for White.

Ruy Lopez (Main Line, continued)

The main line (1.e4 e5 2.Nf3 Nc6 3.Bb5 a6 4.Ba4 Nf6 5.O-O Be7 6.Re1 b5 7.Bb3 O-O) remains the most often played moves.

8.c3

White's whole strategy has been geared toward commanding the center and establishing a Classical Pawn Center.

This is another major theoretical crossroad for Black. He has the fantastically complex choice of the Marshall Gambit, 8...d5, or he can play the main line, 8...d6.

Ruy Lopez Marshall Gambit

One of America's strongest players was the renowned Frank James Marshall (1877–1944). Marshall was a wonderfully inventive player who came up with a number of attacking ideas. He will forever be immortalized due to his discovery of the *Marshall Gambit*. According to legend, Marshall would sleep with a pencil and paper by his bedside so that in case he woke up in the middle of the night, he could quickly scribble down his inspiration. "You never know when you might get an idea," he would intone.

In 1909, Marshall was recognized as one of the top players in the world when he agreed to play an exhibition match against the then-unknown Cuban chess talent, Jose Raul Capablanca (1888–1942, World Champion 1921–27). The match was to be a tune-up for the well-known veteran, and the whole chess world was shocked when Capablanca soundly thrashed Marshall by the one-sided score of 8–1 with 14 draws. (In 1921, Capablanca would become World Champion by defeating Emanuel Lasker.) For Marshall, his loss to Capablanca was a heartfelt one and he prepared his revenge. Marshall came up with the idea for his gambit and spent the intervening years waiting for the moment to spring his surprise upon Capablanca. In 1918 the perfect circumstances presented themselves, and Capablanca fell right into Marshall's surprise weapon. However, many years of diligent preparation couldn't match the natural

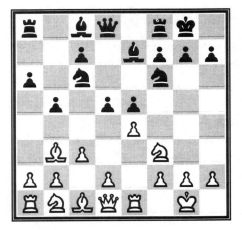

DIAGRAM 44.

talents of Capablanca. Over the board, Capablanca played a near-perfect game and won! Marshall Gambit games have been played ever since.

The Marshall Gambit is reached by (1.e4 e5 2.Nf3 Nc6 3.Bb5 a6 4.Ba4 Nf6 5.O-O Be7 6.Re1 b5 7.Bb3 O-O 8.c3):

8...d5

Diagram 44 shows the current position.

Based on the principles I've described, this move is a fine one—except that Black loses a pawn in freeing his game. Is it worth it? Play is now forced:

9.exd5 Nxd5   10.Nxe5 Nxe5

11.Rxe5 c6!

Marshall's original idea was 11...Nf6, aiming at ...Nf6-g4 and ...Be7-d6 with an attack on the h2-pawn. Later it was discovered that the d5-Knight sits on a fine square and should stay put as Black wants to play ...Be7-d6 and ...Qd8-h4, leaping to the attack. The most common moves are 12.d4 Bd6 13.Re1 Qh4 14.g3 Qh3 15.Be3, with countless games being played. Go to your local library, check out a book on the Marshall Gambit, and enrich your knowledge of this fascinating gambit.

Ruy Lopez (Main Line, continued)

Not every player likes to gambit a pawn, especially as Black. While the Marshall Gambit is a fearsome weapon, preference is usually given to the solid (1.e4 e5 2.Nf3 Nc6 3.Bb5 a6 4.Ba4 Nf6 5.O-O Be7 6.Re1 b5 7.Bb3 O-O 8.c3):

8...d6

Black takes a stand in the center, protects his e5-pawn, and prepares to develop his Queenside pieces. White now plays a paradoxical move as his main choice:

9.h3!?

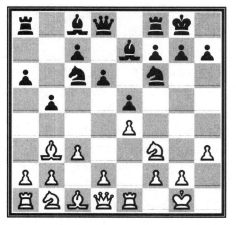

Diagram 45 shows the position and draws us to my next principle:

> *Every opening move should have a purpose. Most opening moves should be motivated by one of the following reasons:*

DIAGRAM 45.

- ■ *Capturing a piece or pawn*

- ■ *Avoiding the loss of a piece or pawn*

- ■ *Protecting the King*

- ■ *Playing for the control of the sweet center*

Of the four reasons in this principle, the one that most often guides opening decisions is playing to control the sweet center. Capturing, retreating, and protecting the King will become second nature. Such moves are made automatically and are in the minority. Controlling the center motivates most moves. With this in mind, how can White's ninth move of the main line Ruy Lopez be the culmination of centuries of master games? Certainly, 9.h3 doesn't fit with any of my principles and it might even be argued that this move even weakens the King's pawn shield. Why waste a precious tempo on such a move?

White's opening moves are guided by his desire to control the center. For some time he has been winding up for the move d2-d4. Why didn't White just play it? After 9.d4 Bg4!, White faces an awkward pin upon his f3-Knight. This pin in turn puts pressure upon White's center. Many games have continued with 10.Be3 Na5! (10...Nxe4? 11.Bd5 wins a piece—another trap worth remembering!) 11.Bc2 (11.dxe5 Bxf3 is considered an even game) 11…Nc4, and Black has proven to have an equal position.

As this straightforward try failed to prove an advantage, White players tried another tack: 1.e4 e5 2.Nf3 Nc6 3.Bb5 a6 4.Ba4 Nf6 5.O-O Be7 6.Re1 b5 7.Bb3 O-O 8.c3 d6 9.d4 Bg4 10.d5. In this way, White achieves a central pawn wedge. It took some time, but the way to an even position was discovered: 10…Na5 11.Bc2 c6! 12.h3 Bc8! 13.dxc6 Qc7! After this series of precise defensive moves, Black would recapture the c6-pawn with good piece play. Dissatisfied by the effects of the annoying pin, …Bc8-g4, White spent a whole tempo stopping it.

Diagram 45 is too rich in its choices for Black. It would take a series of opening books just to get through them all. I'm choosing but one and calling it the main line. First let me list popular alternative moves to the main line.

- 9…h6
- 9…Bb7
- 9…Be6
- 9…a5
- 9…Re8
- 9…Nd7

Each of these alternative moves has something unique about it, which makes them all worthy of study. To my mind, the most consequent choice is:

9…Na5

Anticipating that White will one day push his d-pawn up the board, Black's Knight gets out of the way while seeking to push the b3-Bishop to a less powerful diagonal.

10.Bc2

White gets the hint and retreats his Bishop to safety. In general, grand-masters are quite protective of their Bishops and prefer them to Knights.

10…c5!

This was Black's deeper plan. He brings another pawn into the battle for supremacy of the sweet center. Note how often the players aspire to attack the sweet center.

11.d4!

At long last, after what seemed like lengthy delays, White has established his classical center and now seeks to complete his development. The first piece of happy news is that Black's e5-pawn is now under attack.

11...Qc7

Having first developed a number of his pieces, Black feels the time has come to introduce his Queen into battle. Black defends the e5-pawn and begins a little pressure along the c-file. His goal is to harass the c2-Bishop.

12.Nbd2

White develops a Knight, with the intent of maneuvering over to the Kingside in a classic Ruy Lopez.

12...Bd7

Black has to carefully choose where he wants to develop his Bishop. Both 12...Bb7 and 12...Be6 invite 13.d5, shutting off the Bishop's future. Black chooses this safe square and vacates the c8-square for a Rook.

13.Nf1

White continues to redirect his Knight toward the Kingside. From there, he can use the g3-square to jump to the f5-outpost, or he can use the e3-square with the option for the d5-outpost.

White's last move leads to Diagram 46 and the end of this survey of classical King Pawn openings. The ideas and plans shared should leave you with the impression that while there is much to learn, the *ideas*

DIAGRAM 46.

behind the moves are easy to understand, especially when you consider the principles of opening play.

> **SOLUTION.** The problem for White after 1.e4 e5 2.Nf3 Nc6 3.Bb5 a6 4.Ba4 Nf6 5.O-O Be7 6.Nc3 b5 7.Bb3 O-O 8.d4? is that 8…exd4 9.Nxd4? Nxd4 10.Qxd4 c5! 11.Qc3 c4! snares White's b3-Bishop. A pattern worth remembering!

Classical Queen Pawn Openings

I n the same manner as I did in Chapter Three, in this chapter I survey classical Queen Pawn openings and their defenses. I'll follow a main line while considering a large number of deviations along the way. At all times, I'll discuss the fundamental ideas and the principles involved.

Queen Pawn openings, as their name suggests, begin with White moving the pawn in front of his Queen:

1.d4

Proponents of 1.d4 make an excellent argument for their favorite opening move. White's d-pawn strikes and occupies the sweet center, avenues for both the Bishop and Queen are opened, and the pawn is *supported* by White's Queen. Recall that in Chapter Three, White's e4-pawn was constantly besieged and required protection. In Queen Pawn openings, the d4-pawn has built-in protection.

Proponents of 1.e4 make a counterargument: 1.d4 doesn't help the development of White's Kingside forces and White's King must remain in the center for at least an extra tempo or two. So you must weigh the pros and cons in making an opening choice.

Using Steinitz's theory of equilibrium, Black's reply is expected:

1...d5

Black establishes a pawn in the center and stakes a claim to White's e4 and c4-squares. How is White to follow up? White has four main options, which I discuss in turn:

■ 2.Nc3 (Chigorin Variation)

■ 2.Bf4 (Mason Variation)

■ 2.Bg5 (Levitsky Variation)

■ 2.c4 (Queen's Gambit), the main line

Chigorin Variation

White has taken several approaches in playing for control of the center, including:

2.Nc3

White plays directly in the center, trying for e2-e4 and quick development. This move is called the *Chigorin Variation*. If White is able to play e2-e4, the variation works well for White and he gains an advantage. Black can put a stop to White's plans by:

2...Nf6

This makes it difficult for White to reinforce his control over the e4-square. White now has two direct choices:

■ 3.Bg5 (Richter Attack)

■ 3.e4 (Blackmar-Diemer Gambit)

DIAGRAM 47.

Richter Attack

The *Richter Attack* begins (1.d4 d5 2.Nc3 Nf6):

3.Bg5

As shown in Diagram 47, White's aim is to eliminate the f6-Knight so that he can play e2-e4 with a lion's share of the center.

Black can respond to this aggressive try with 3...Bf5, developing a Bishop while covering the e4-square; or 3...Nbd7, defending the f6-Knight.

3...Bf5

Black should expect White to sacrifice a pawn and to try to force through e2-e4. Often the f5-Bishop becomes a target.

4.f3

White revs up for his central push and Black doesn't have an easy choice to make. If he tries 4...e6?, 5.e4! will be powerful due to the pinned f6-Knight. Black must play:

4...Nbd7

Black's Bishop development is premature.

5.e4 dxe4

6.Bc4

White's lead in development leads to a dangerous gambit. This line is particularly potent against beginning players.

The Chigorin Variation in combination with the Richter Attack (1.d4 d5 2.Nc3 Nf6 3.Bg5) is not to be trifled with, and Black has to play with care. I prefer the second choice for Black:

3...Nbd7!

4.f3

Once more White winds up for his center push.

4...c5!

Black responds with his own counter in the center.

5.dxc5

White could play the defensive 5.e3, but this negates his strategy of playing for e2-e4. Black would play 5...e6 with a fine game. Neither would the immediate 5.e4 cxd4 6.Qxd4 e5! work, when Black has seized the center and has the better position.

5...e6

Black prepares to recapture the c5-pawn.

6.e4

White completes his plan but at a cost. Black's counter in the center has been quite timely.

6...Bxc5

7.exd5

White has won a pawn but his position is weakened on the g1-a7 diagonal. By continuing:

7...Qb6

Black has the superior position.

Blackmar-Diemer Gambit

Clearly, Black can handle the Richter Attack (1.d4 d5 2.Nc3 Nf6 3.Bg5 Nbd7!) with confidence. Therefore a favorite continuation of club players is the *Blackmar-Diemer Gambit* (1.d4 d5 2.Nc3 Nf6):

3.e4

White immediately gambits a central pawn for quick development. Black should not be intimidated; he has played two reasonable opening moves and collects the offering.

3...dxe4

4.f3

White attacks the e4-pawn in order to continue his development.

4...exf3

5.Nxf3 Bg4

White has a slight lead in development and open lines for his pieces. It is doubtful that he has full compensation for the pawn. Nevertheless, the Blackmar-Diemer Gambit remains a favorite.

Mason and Levitsky Variations

Besides developing his Queen Knight on move two, White has also tried developing his Queen Bishop by (1.d4 d5) 2.Bf4 (the *Mason Variation*) and 2.Bg5 (the *Levitsky Variation*). Both of these moves have as their aim setting up a solid central position with e2-e3. White wants to first develop his Bishop outside the pawn chain (f2, e3, and d4). The problem with both these moves is that they don't put sufficient pressure on Black's center. By proceeding cautiously, Black obtains a fine game:

2.Bf4 Bf5   3.e3 e6

4.c4

White tries to disturb Black in the center. Without this move, Black would just play ...Bf8-d6 with a balanced game. But in view of what happens, the text is too risky for White.

4...Bxb1!

In a surprising move, Black trades a developed piece for an undeveloped one. But Black's plan of ...Bf8-b4+ is quite strong.

5.Qa4+

Aware of Black's threat of 5...Bb4+, White first tries to guard the b4-square before capturing the Bishop.

5...Nc6   6.Rxb1 Bb4+

7.Kd1 Bd6!

Diagram 48 shows that White cannot castle, and Black can face the future with confidence.

Similarly, the Levitsky Variation (1.d4 d5 2.Bg5) isn't much of a problem for Black. Black can play:

2...Nf6

3.Bxf6 exf6

With the two Bishops for the dou-
bled pawns, Black has the advan-
tage. Or he can try the aggressive:

2...f6

3.Bh4 Nh6

Black lays plans to eliminate
White's h4-Bishop by playing
...Nh6-f5.

DIAGRAM 48.

Queen's Gambit (Main Line)

By an overwhelming margin, White's favored second move is:

2.c4

White immediately attacks the d5-pawn and threatens to capture and eliminate Black's center. By commencing the *Queen's Gambit,* White hopes to entice Black into capturing the c4-pawn, and after a subsequent recapture, White would then have a lead in development. The Queen's Gambit is shown in Diagram 49.

If White is allowed to play c4xd5 unimpeded, Black's center is destroyed. Black has several choices:

- 2...dxc4 (Queen's Gambit Accepted)
- 2...c6 (Slav Defense)
- 2...e6 (Queen's Gambit Declined), the main line
- 2...Bf5 (Grau Variation)
- 2...Nc6 (Chigorin Defense)

Queen's Gambit Accepted

DIAGRAM 49.

The *Queen's Gambit Accepted* (QGA) follows White's plan of knocking Black's d5-pawn out of the center. Play begins (1.d4 d5 2.c4):

2...dxc4

White can play 3.Qa4+, immediately recapturing the c4-pawn. But this action causes a premature development of White's Queen. It is better for White to try to recapture the c4-pawn with the f1-Bishop. The simplest move is:

3.e3

A key alternative is 3.e4. Expanding upon the same idea, White gains a larger share of the center. The problem with this is that Black is also quick to react in the center: 3...e5 attacks the d4-pawn. After 4.Nf3 (it is a mistake to try to win the e5-pawn with 4.dxe5? Qxd1+ 5.Kxd1 Nc6, when Black gets a good position) 4...exd4 5.Nxd4 Nf6, Black has an even game.

In the QGA, Black usually allows White to recapture the c4-pawn. He hopes that he too will attack the center with his own ...c7-c5 to reestablish the equilibrium.

3...Nf6
4.Bxc4

White has accomplished his goal: The d5-pawn has been removed and he has gained a lead in development. Play usually proceeds:

4...e6   5.Nf3 c5
6.O-O

Diagram 50 pictures the main position of the QGA. White has a lead in development, which gives him an advantage. Black aims to equalize by trading pawns on the d4-square. The QGA is an excellent defense for those players who like to counterattack. Its drawback is that if White plays accurately, he will keep an advantage for a long while.

Slav Defense

One of the most solid defenses to the Queen Pawn opening is the *Slav Defense,* which was favored by Vasily Smyslov (1921–, World Champion 1957–58) and Mikhail Botvinnik (1911–95, World Champion 1948–57, 1958–60, 1961–63). The Slav Defense begins (1.d4 d5 2.c4):

2...c6

DIAGRAM 50.

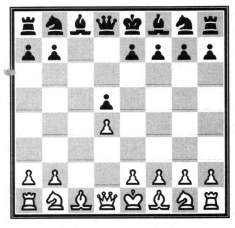

DIAGRAM 51.

Black bolsters his d-pawn and offers White a symmetrical position after:

3.cxd5 cxd5

This position, shown in Diagram 51, is known as the *Slav Defense Exchange Variation*. White has a small advantage in having an extra tempo for development.

4.Nc3 Nf6   5.Nf3 Nc6 6.Bf4

This results in a slightly better position for White. When confronted with the Slav Defense, many players prefer not to trade central pawns. They reason that the c6-pawn blocks Black's b8-Knight from the useful c6-square. However, if White decides not to trade pawns on the d5-square, he has to keep an eye out that Black doesn't capture the c4-pawn and then play ...b7-b5, keeping the pawn forever.

The preferred way to meet the Slav Defense (1.d4 d5 2.c4 c6) is to protect the c4 and d4-pawns with:

DIAGRAM 52.

3.e3 Nf6   4.Nc3 e6 5.Nf3 Nbd7

Diagram 52 shows the position reached. This line of the Slav Defense is known as the *Merano Variation*. It is an extremely rich and fascinating position preferred by the young lions on the international chess circuit. Black intends to play ...d5xc4 and ...b7-b5-b4, with play similar to the QGA.

Besides choosing the Merano Variation, White can also play (1.d4 d5 2.c4 c6):

3.Nc3

This leaves Black with the choice of 3...dxc4 or 3...Nf6. The latter is the most common choice. But White has to be aware that 3...dxc4 4.e4 (the *Alekhine Variation)* b5 5.a4 b4 6.Na2 e5 leads to a very sharp position, for which he should be prepared!

3...Nf6

White often keeps the tension in the position by playing:

4.Nf3

Once again Black faces a crossroad. Should he capture the c4-pawn with 4...dxc4 or reinforce his center once more with 4...e6 (the Semi-Slav Defense)? This decision seems to be an even split.

4...dxc4

Diagram 53 shows the current position. Black's capture is what gives the Slav Defense its unique flavor. Black intends to play ...b7-b5, hanging on to the captured c4-pawn.

5.a4

With this move, the *Alapin Variation,* White prevents the protection of the c4-pawn. Play now proceeds:

5...Bf5	**6.e3 e6**
7.Bxc4 Bb4	**8.O-O O-O**

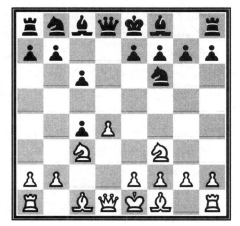

DIAGRAM 53.

White, with a slight advantage, will try for the central break e3-e4, but for the moment, Black controls the e4-square.

Besides the Alapin Variation, White can sacrifice a pawn (1.d4 d5 2.c4 c6 3.Nc3 Nf6 4.Nf3 dxc4):

5.e4

White doesn't prevent ...b7-b5 and instead grabs the center.

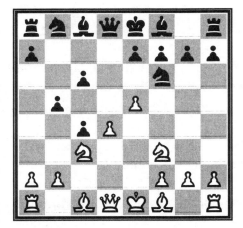

DIAGRAM 54.

5...b5
6.e5
This is called the *Geller Gambit,* which is shown in Diagram 54. Play continues:

6...Nd5
7.a4
White has a grip in the center but is a pawn behind. After a great deal of practice, theorists consider Black's position to be sound.

Semi-Slav Defense

Besides the ...d5xc4 capture which distinguishes the Slav Defense, Black can also play the *Semi-Slav Defense* (1.d4 d5 2.c4 c6 3.Nc3 Nf6 4.Nf3):

4...e6
Black reinforces the d5-pawn. White could play 5.e3, which transposes into the Merano Variation, or continue with the aggressive:

5.Bg5
White develops his Bishop and threatens to play e2-e4, now that the f6-Knight is pinned. This move, the *Anti-Merano Game,* is the prelude to one of the most difficult theoretical puzzles in chess:

5...dxc4
Black decides that the time is now ripe to capture the c4-pawn. White's move is expected:

6.e4
White grabs the center and is primed to capture the c4-pawn with a large lead in development.

6...b5
Black holds onto his c4-pawn.

7.e5

Taking advantage of the pinned f6-Knight, White threatens to win a piece. Black has to break the h4-d8 pin.

7...h6   8.Bh4 g5
9.Nxg5!

White isn't about to allow the pin to be broken.

9...hxg5
10.Bxg5 Nbd7

This is the *Semi-Slav, Botvinnik Gambit*. Diagram 55 shows the position.

Black is temporarily up a pawn,

DIAGRAM 55.

which White will soon recapture. Current opening theory now continues:

11.g3 Bb7   12.Bg2 Qb6
13.exf6 O-O-O 14.O-O

Black has sacrificed a pawn for a Queenside majority, open lines on the Kingside, and play in the center. The resulting position is one of the sharpest positions in opening theory. The world's highest-rated player, Garry Kasparov, has played some sparkling games in this variation.

Queen's Gambit Declined (Main Line, continued)

The oldest line in the classical Queen Pawn openings is the *Queen's Gambit Declined* (QGD), which begins (1.d4 d5 2.c4):

2...e6

Black protects the d5-pawn and prepares to develop his Kingside pieces. The problem with this move is the obvious plight of the c8-Bishop. It is now locked inside Black's pawn chain and will remain inactive for some time.

Grau Variation

While the QGD is a solid defensive choice, players have looked for ways of activating their c8-Bishop before committing their e-pawn. The most common tries for Black are 2...Bf5 (the Grau Variation) and 2...Nc6 (the Chigorin Defense).

The Grau Variation begins (1.d4 d5 2.c4):

2...Bf5

Black develops a Bishop and controls the sweet center, but this move has a tactical drawback that earns White an advantage. This allows a moment to introduce another opening principle:

Develop your Knights before developing your Bishops.

This is a principle that is easily violated and not so easily punished. For this reason, many chess teachers don't emphasize this principle. Neither do I. Nonetheless it is a principle worth knowing—even if you don't pay strict attention to it. The idea of the principle is that in the early opening, you're not sure how the position will shape up. Will a diagonal remain open or closed? Will the Bishop have to move again soon? Sometimes, as in the Ruy Lopez, the Bishop move on move three is considered White's best. Other times, as in the Mason and Levitsky Variations, the Bishop moves seem premature. In the Blackmar-Diemer Gambit, Black must be very careful in developing his c8-Bishop.

In the Grau Variation, White is quick to take the d5-pawn:

3.cxd5!

This is stronger than 3.Nc3 e6 (now Black is comfortable playing this move) 4.Qb3 Nc6 5.e3 Bb4, when White has only a small advantage.

3...Bxb1

Black moves his developed Bishop yet again. The move is actually forced, as 3...Qxd5? 4.Nc3 will be a quick disaster. Black's Queen is attacked and is forced to move again. Further, White will soon play e2-e4, grabbing the center and developing with tempo.

4.Qa4+!

Only this move, which violates the principle of not developing the Queen early, gives White the advantage. After the recapture 4.Rxb1 Qxd5, Black's Queen has taken up a stable square in the center. The a2-pawn is attacked and Black can face the future with confidence. The Grau Variation is particularly effective against beginning players who won't see the necessity of White's fourth move.

4...c6

Black makes a forced response. After 4...Qd7 5.Qxd7+ Nxd7 6.Rxb1 Ngf6 7.Bd2 Nb6 8.f3! Nbxd5 9.e4, White has gained the advantage with his two Bishops and a classical pawn center.

5.Rxb1

White recaptures the b1-Bishop. He can also consider 5.dxc6 Nxc6 6.Rxb1 e5! 7.Bd2 (to prevent ...Bf8-b4+, which would be quite unpleasant!) 7...exd4 8.g3, with a slight advantage for White.

5...Qxd5   6.Nf3 Nd7

7.Bd2

White must avoid 7.Bf4?? Qe4!, which launches a double attack against the f4-Bishop and b1-Rook.

7...Ngf6

8.e3

Diagram 56 shows the current position, where White has an advantage due to his two Bishops and superior central control.

DIAGRAM 56.

Chigorin Defense

An altogether different and tricky problem is presented by the *Chigorin Defense* (1.d4 d5 2.c4):

2...Nc6

Black plays for piece play and an open game. Unconcerned with the fight for the d5-square, Black plays for a counterattack against the d4-pawn and seeks to play ...e7-e5 with an explosion in the center. White's most reliable reaction is to cover the e5-square.

3.Nf3 Bg4

Black intensifies the fight for the e5-square.

4.cxd5

White strips Black of his central bulwark. Black must play energetically to stay in the battle.

4...Bxf3!

This move weakens the protection of the d4-pawn. Weaker is 4...Qxd5 5.Nc3, which gives White a nice advantage.

5.gxf3

After 5.dxc6 Bxc6, Black is doing well. He isn't behind in development and he has control over the sweet center.

5...Qxd5

6.e3

White would dearly love to play 6.Nc3, developing with tempo, but first he must fortify the d4-pawn.

DIAGRAM 57.

6...e5!

7.Nc3! Bb4!

Diagram 57 reveals excellent play by both sides.

Black is fighting to avoid the loss of a tempo with his Queen.

8.Bd2 Bxc3

9.bxc3 Nge7

White has a broad center and the two Bishops. White's position is considered to be better, but Black will have play against White's doubled pawns. His aim is to play ...Ne7-g6-h4. The Chigorin remains a viable defense worthy of study.

Queen's Gambit Declined (Main Line, continued)

The Queen's Gambit Declined (1.d4 d5 2.c4 e6) has been a favored defense of nearly every World Champion. That fact alone is enough to convince me of its soundness. White has a hard time knocking out the d5-pawn and he immediately puts pressure on this pawn.

3.Nc3

This is the most aggressive move. White can also play 3.Nf3, which often transposes into the main line.

Catalan Variation

A crucial alternative at this juncture is:

3.g3

White prepares to *fianchetto* his f1-Bishop so that it can pressure the d5-pawn. The idea of a fianchetto is considered a modern concept. Classical players preferred to leave their Kingside pawns on their original squares so that after castling, the Kingside has no weak squares. (I'll discuss the Kingside fianchetto at length in later chapters.) I'm quite fond of this third move, which introduces the *Catalan Variation*. White's f1-Bishop will move to the long diagonal h1-a8, which intensifies White's pressure in the sweet center.

The drawback of the Catalan is that White's c4-pawn no longer receives the protection of the f1-Bishop. Thus, if Black captures the c4-pawn, White will have to find another piece to recapture with. Black can meet the Catalan by capturing the c4-pawn with ...d5xc4 (the *Open Catalan*) or by blocking the long diagonal with ...c7-c6 (the *Closed Catalan*).

Open Catalan Variation

Deciding to capture the c4-pawn is a sensible reaction because the c4-pawn lacks protection.

3...dxc4

White intends to recapture the pawn soon. First he completes the fianchetto:

4.Bg2

White shouldn't be too anxious to recapture the pawn; 4.Qa4+ Bd7 5.Qxc4 Bc6 6.Nf3 Bxf3! 7.exf3 Nc6 8.Be3 Qd5! leaves a fine game for Black.

4...Nf6

Black proceeds with his development. He can also consider 4...c5 5.Qa4+ Bd7 6.Qxc4 Bc6 with approximate equality.

5.Nf3

After 5.Qa4+ Nbd7 6.Qxc4 c5, it is highly likely that the game will transpose to the line we are investigating.

5...Be7

This is the solid choice for Black because he intends quick castling. Black has also tried 5...c5, 5...Nc6, and 5...a6. These enterprising alternatives aim to retain the captured c4-pawn.

6.O-O O-O

7.Qa4

At last White decides it is time to recapture the c4-pawn. In the tempi that it costs White to complete this task, Black aims to neutralize White's fianchetto with one of his own.

7...a6!

Black threatens to secure the c4-pawn with ...b7-b5.

8.Qxc4 b5

9.Qc2 Bb7

In Diagram 58, we see a key starting position of the Open Catalan. Many games have been contested from this position with White playing 10.Bd2, 10.Bf4, and 10.Bg5 as his most popular choices.

The battle lines are fairly simple: White will try to establish a classical pawn center and outposts on the c5 and e5-squares. Black will play for ...c7-c5, trying to create a symmetrical pawn structure and an equal game.

Closed Catalan Variation

The Closed Catalan is designed to keep the long diagonal blocked. It begins (1.d4 d5 2.c4 e6 3.g3):

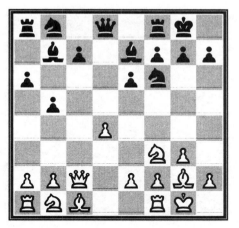

DIAGRAM 58.

3...c6

Black hopes that in this way the g2-Bishop will bite on granite. Black's last move, however, contains a trace of poison. White must be watchful for a change of plans by Black. He might grab the c4-pawn and then play ...b7-b5, holding the extra pawn as in the Slav Defense. Worried for the safety of the c4-pawn, White plays:

4.Qc2

Although White is uncomfortable moving his Queen so early, the Queen isn't easily attacked. White has to be aware of a dangerous trap in this line. White can't just play 4.b3? to defend the c4-pawn, because after 4...dxc4 5.bxc4? Bb4+!, White will lose the d4-pawn.

4...Nf6

Black has another major choice at this moment. He can radically change the complexion of the game by trying to control the e4-square.

Dutch Stonewall Defense

What a marvelous name for a defense: the *Dutch Stonewall.* Just as the name implies, Black creates a fortress of pawns (d5, f5, c6, and e6) in the center and plays for control over the e4-square. Play begins (1.d4 d5 2.c4 e6 3.g3 c6 4.Qc2):

4...f5

DIAGRAM 59.

Diagram 59 shows the position after Black's fourth move. Clearly, White is going to have a hard time liberating the center with e2-e4, but on the other hand, Black has created a hole, the e5-square, which beckons a White Knight.

Play usually proceeds:

5.Nf3 Nf6   6.Bg2 Bd6
7.Bf4

Despite the blocked nature of the position, White has the advantage because he has a superior Bishop and more space. The Dutch Stonewall Defense remains a favorite of amateur players because the ideas for the defender are simple to follow. Trade the pieces that land on the e5-square and move your pieces to the Kingside.

Closed Catalan Variation, continued

While the Dutch Stonewall is an intriguing defense, most players prefer

DIAGRAM 60.

not to commit their f-pawn so early. In the Closed Catalan (1.d4 d5 2.c4 e6 3.g3 c6 4.Qc2 Nf6), Black aims for quiet development.

5.Bg2 Be7   6.Nf3 O-O
7.O-O

Both players aim to complete their development. Black has a problem of what to do with the c8-Bishop. It's stuck inside his pawn chain, blocked behind the e6-pawn, as shown in Diagram 60.

QUIZ. How would you try to activate the c8-Bishop? The solution is at the end of this chapter.

Queen's Gambit Declined (Main Line, continued)

At this moment in the QGD main line (1.d4 d5 2.c4 e6 3.Nc3), Black can play 3...c6, transposing back to a Slav Defense, or he can play 3...f5 with a Dutch Stonewall. Because White has developed a Knight hitting the e4-square and the d5-pawn, Black opposes him with a similar scheme:

3...Nf6

Black tries to invite White to trade pawns on the d5-square. Such a trade would benefit Black for the moment! Why? If White tries 4.cxd5 exd5, then Black's c8-Bishop would no longer be blocked and its development would be unimpeded.

Tarrasch Defense

Because Black is trying to provoke a trade of central pawns, one of the definitive practitioners of classical chess, Siegbert Tarrasch (1862–1934), devised the Tarrasch Defense, which begins (1.d4 d5 2.c4 e6 3.Nc3):

3...c5

From the perspective of fighting for central control, Black's reaction is quite sensible. (See Diagram 61.) White can play 4.e3 Nf6 5.Nf3 Nc6,

DIAGRAM 61.

91

producing a symmetrical position with White having the move. In general, this line of play offers White only a minimal advantage. Therefore, on move four, White's main line is to capture in the center:

4.cxd5

Black should be pleased at having provoked this capture. He now has to decide between 4...cxd4 (the *Schara-Hennig Gambit*) and the usual 4...exd5, recapturing in the center.

Schara-Hennig Gambit

The Schara-Hennig Gambit is an excellent weapon for beginning players. Black aims for rapid piece development (1.d4 d5 2.c4 e6 3.Nc3 c5 4.cxd5):

4...cxd4

This capture provokes White's Queen to develop early so that Black can attack it with gain of tempi.

5.Qxd4 Nc6!

This is Black's key move. The d5-pawn is pinned and White has to move the Queen.

Diagram 62 shows the position and how Black's Knight is developed with tempo. White withdraws the Queen:

DIAGRAM 62.

6.Qd1 exd5

7.Qxd5

White has won a pawn but has made several moves with the Queen, which has cost him time.

7...Bd7

Black continues developing while preparing ...Ng8-f6, also with tempo. Black has tried 7...Be6 8.Qxd8+ Rxd8. Black's play displays the results of a classical gambit. Although Black is a pawn down, its sacrifice has been for quick development. Still, White is considered to have an advantage in this middle game position.

8.e3 Nf6

9.Qb3

White will try hard to catch up in development while Black will try to coordinate an attack. Practice favors White.

Tarrasch Defense, continued

For those players who don't like to gambit pawns as Black, the Tarrasch Defense (1.d4 d5 2.c4 e6 3.Nc3 c5 4.cxd5) is the natural reaction.

4...exd5

White has tried a large number of moves here:

- ■ 5.e4!? dxe4 6.d5 is the Marshall Gambit. Leave it to Frank Marshall to find gambits for both White and Black. White is playing for fast development and this gambit is a dangerous one for the second player.

- ■ White can force Black to sacrifice a pawn by 5.dxc5?! d4! 6.Na4. This is the Tarrasch Gambit, and after the theoretical recommendation 6...b5 7.cxb6 axb6, the poorly placed a4-Knight gives Black an excellent position.

- ■ The most common moves are 5.Nf3 Nc6. Black reinforces the pressure on the d4-pawn. White can now try 6.e3 Nf6 7.Bb5 cxd4 8.Nxd4 Bd7, which is slightly better for White. Or he can play the popular fianchetto variation, called the *Schlechter Variation:* 6.g3 Nf6 7.Bg2 Be7 8.O-O O-O 9.Bg5. This is shown in Diagram 63.

DIAGRAM 63.

Modern practice has shown an advantage for White due to the pressure that White's pieces have in the center. From Tarrasch's view as a classical player, he was certain that Black had achieved an equal game. The Tarrasch Defense was a favorite of Garry Kasparov during his early career.

Queen's Gambit Declined (Main Line, continued)

White now has several moves available that very often transpose to one another. After 1.d4 d5 2.c4 e6 3.Nc3 Nf6, he can try:

- ■ 4.cxd5, the *Exchange Variation*. The Exchange Variation can be played at nearly any moment in the moves ahead, but it is best delayed for the moment.

- ■ 4.Nf3. After ...Nbd7, White confronts the same issues as before. On which square will he develop the c1-Bishop? 5.Bf4 only encourages 5...Bb4, which puts White on the defensive. White's best move is therefore 5.Bg5, which is very close to the main line. For the sake of accuracy, I'll play the correct order of moves.

- ■ 4.Bg5, the main line. Most opening theorists today believe that 4.Bg5 is the most effective. I agree with them.

(Besides these main moves, White can also play 4.Bf4, which misplaces the Bishop. After 4...Bb4!, Black pins the c3-Knight and intends a quick ...c7-c5 and ...Qd8-a5 attack. The development of the f4-Bishop doesn't help White counter Black's plans.)

My preferred order of moves is (1.d4 d5 2.c4 e6 3.Nc3 Nf6):

4.Bg5

This move (see Diagram 64) makes a lot more sense than the alternatives. The defending f6-Knight is pinned, and White immediately threatens its capture and, if possible, the win of the d5-pawn. To defend against this possibility Black's two main defenses are 4...Be7 (the Tartakover Variation) and 4...Nbd7 (the main line).

Tartakover Variation

Chess theorists are evenly split between Tartakover and main line adherents. The *Tartakover Variation* begins (1.d4 d5 2.c4 e6 3.Nc3 Nf6 4.Bg5):

4...Be7

Black prepares to quickly castle while breaking the pin on the f6-Knight.

5.e3 O-O

White must make a fundamental decision. Does he intend to delay

DIAGRAM 64.

the development of his g1-Knight with moves such as 6.Qd2, 6.Qc2, or 6.Rc1—or simply develop the Knight? Each of these moves contains its own peculiarities and Black must be familiar with each of them. Because developing the g1-Knight is the most natural, I'll follow that line:

6.Nf3

This leaves Black with the choice of:

- 6...Ne4 (Lasker Defense)

- 6...h6 (Neo-Orthodox Defense)

- 6...b6 (Orthodox Defense)

Lasker Defense

A favorite defense of former World Champion Emanuel Lasker was (1.d4 d5 2.c4 e6 3.Nc3 Nf6 4.Bg5 Be7 5.e3 O-O 6.Nf3):

6...Ne4

This defense now bears his name. Black's plan is to trade a few minor pieces and gain a reasonable position.

7.Bxe7 Qxe7

DIAGRAM 65.

Diagram 65 shows the *Lasker Defense*. White can choose 8.Nxe4 dxe4 9.Nd2 f5, which is considered about equal. Or he can choose 8.cxd5 Nxc3 9.bxc3 exd5 10.c4, which is slightly better for White. With the main move, White develops a Rook and defends the c3-Knight:

8.Rc1 Nxc3	**9.Rxc3 c6**
10.Bd3 dxc4	**11.Bxc4 b6**

This line provides a small advantage to White.

Neo-Orthodox Defense

The *Neo-Orthodox Defense* begins (1.d4 d5 2.c4 e6 3.Nc3 Nf6 4.Bg5 Be7 5.e3 O-O 6.Nf3):

6...h6

This puts the question to White's Bishop: Will he exchange Bishop for Knight or move away? (The reason for the strange name, "neo," is that while Black is playing an Orthodox Defense, the idea of inserting the move ...h7-h6 is relatively modern. Classical players didn't like weakening their Kingside.)

7.Bh4 b6

Following the usual retreat, Black decides to fianchetto his c8-Bishop as in the Closed Catalan. This variation is called the *Tartakover, Makogonov, Bondarevsky Variation*. A mouthful you say? That's why its also called the *TMB Variation*.

I discuss this position (see Diagram 66) and its strategies extensively in *Winning Chess Brilliancies* (Microsoft Press, 1995), on pages 2–15. In this game (Robert James Fischer versus Boris Spassky, Reykjavik 1972, Game 6), Black retains a solid central position.

Queen's Gambit Declined (Main Line, continued)

Return now to the main line (1.d4 d5 2.c4 e6 3.Nc3 Nf6 4.Bg5):

4...Nbd7

Black will try to provoke the trade c4xd5 ...e6xd5, so that the c8-Bishop will develop on the c8-h3 diagonal. With Black's fourth move, he reinforces his f6-Knight, the defender of the d5-pawn.

DIAGRAM 66.

5.e3

White prepares further development.

How many players have fallen into the cunning trap 5.cxd5 exd5 6.Nxd5?? White has thought that he has won a pawn due to the pin on the f6-Knight. Look at Diagram 67 and see if you can spot White's oversight.

Black continues 6...Nxd5, which has been quite a shock for many. The Knight isn't as badly pinned as first thought! 7.Bxd8 Bb4+! is Black's point. White has to return the Queen. After 8.Qd2 Bxd2+ 9.Kxd2 Kxd8, Black has won a Knight for a pawn and has a winning advantage in force.

White should also avoid: 5.e4?! dxe4 6.Nxe4 h6, which puts the question to White's Bishop at an annoying moment. After the subsequent moves 7.Bxf6 Nxf6, Black has the preferable position.

DIAGRAM 67.

DIAGRAM 68.

5...h6

Black puts the question to White's Bishop. White doesn't benefit from the trade 6.Bxf6 Nxf6, so he retreats the Bishop:

6.Bh4

As seen before, White should avoid 6.Bf4?! Bb4!, which provides good play for Black.

6...Be7

Black commits his Bishop to breaking the pin. Black could also try 6...Bb4, but without the possibility of ...Nf6-e4, such an attack would be premature. Diagram 68 features our main line position.

Now an interesting fight for a tempo ensues. White wants Black to play ...d5xc4 so that he can play Bf1xc4 in one gulp, while Black wants White to play c4xd5 so that after ...e6xd5, a path is cleared for the c8-Bishop. On such nuances the question of an advantage resides. White has two choices:

- 7.cxd5 (Exchange Variation)
- 7.Nf3, the main line

Queen's Gambit Declined, Exchange Variation

If White wants to clarify the pawn structure, then the Queen's Gambit Declined *Exchange Variation* is the preferred choice.

7.cxd5 exd5

8.Bd3

White's Bishops have taken up active squares, but Black has retained a solid central position.

8...c6

Black further cements the center.

9.Nf3

White finally develops his Kingside in preparation for castling. The move 9.Nge2 is appropriately named the *Chameleon Variation*. It is more flexible than 9.Nf3 because it allows a possible f2-f3 and e3-e4 plan, but the Knight is less active on the e2-square.

9...O-O

10.O-O Ne4

This leads to the same trading idea of the Lasker Defense.

DIAGRAM 69.

Diagram 69 shows the position, which is considered a standard one for the Queen's Gambit Exchange. Black intends to hold the e4-square as firmly as possible. Theory considers the Exchange Variation to be only slightly better for White. My view is that Black has an easy game.

Queen's Gambit Declined (Main Line, continued)

Return to the main line (1.d4 d5 2.c4 e6 3.Nc3 Nf6 4.Bg5 Nbd7 5.e3 h6 6.Bh4 Be7):

7.Nf3

Instead of resolving the central tension, White develops a piece and hopes to take advantage of his superior development after 7...dxc4? 8.Bxc4. Black isn't about to aid White's pieces and plays:

7...O-O

Black tucks his King safely onto the Kingside.

8.Rc1

White knows that Black will soon have to develop his c8-Bishop. This means he will try to fianchetto the Bishop or resolve the central tension.

DIAGRAM 70.

White is ready to play down the c-file in either event.

8...a6

Black shows his cards. He intends to capture on the c4-square and then play ...b7-b5, accelerating his Queenside development. The position is shown in Diagram 70.

White must decide if he wants to resolve the center with 9.cxd5 exd5, as in the Queen's Gambit Exchange Variation. He has gained the development move Ra1-c1 in return for the move ...a7-a6, which should give White the advantage. Even so, after 10.Bd3 c6 Black's position is quite solid.

At Diagram 70, White can play 9.a3, still awaiting a resolution in the center. Continuing with 9...dxc4 10.Bxc4 b5 11.Ba2 c5 leaves an approximately equal position.

Having a better understanding of the classical openings makes it easier to understand the modern ones. Although learning the names of the openings and defenses is hardly a requirement, the key to good play is understanding the ideas of central control, quick piece development, and a safe King.

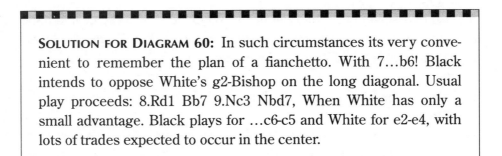

SOLUTION FOR DIAGRAM 60: In such circumstances its very convenient to remember the plan of a fianchetto. With 7...b6! Black intends to oppose White's g2-Bishop on the long diagonal. Usual play proceeds: 8.Rd1 Bb7 9.Nc3 Nbd7, When White has only a small advantage. Black plays for ...c6-c5 and White for e2-e4, with lots of trades expected to occur in the center.

Modern King Pawn Defenses

This chapter, unlike the two previous ones, does not have a "main line" which we plow through while considering alternatives. Instead, it provides a brief sketch of some of the main lines of the more popular modern defenses to White's opening challenge of 1.e4. The Steinitizian principles of equilibrium practically compelled all leading chess players to meet White's opening move in classical style by playing 1...e5. The same was true with Queen Pawn openings when 1.d4 d5 was considered practically forced. Gradually, players began to experiment with a number of different defenses. Their aim was no longer to seek to "establish or re-establish the equilibrium;" in many cases the aim was to attack's White's opening move at once or allow White to occupy the center. There were a large number of experiments and not all of them worked very well! However a number have withstood the test of time. As you follow the openings in this chapter, notice *how both players play for the center, development, and a safe King.* This will be a theme of future chapters.

Alekhine Defense

Sometimes when approaching a game of chess, a player has to be downright surly in his mental attitude (not in personality!) and question the opponent's every move. For a moment, cloak yourself in this same mind frame. White has just played:

1.e4

You haughtily take offense at this move, and you must immediately set about trying to destroy the e4-pawn. You can attack the e4-pawn with moves like ...f7-f5 or ...d7-d5, or you can try to lure it forward to its capture. This is what Alexander Alekhine, fourth World Champion, had in mind when he championed the *Alekhine Defense:*

1...Nf6

This impudent move is shown in Diagram 71.

Black immediately sets out to assault the e4-pawn, with hopes of luring it forward to its doom.

2.e5

White accepts the challenge. He reckons that 2.Nc3 d5 or 2...e5 would not punish Black for his challenge.

2...Nd5

Black's Knight takes up an unstable residence in the middle of the board. The Knight seems to be mocking White's army, daring them to attack.

A horrible debacle would await Black after 2...Ne4? 3.d3! Nc5 4.d4!, when Black's Knight is being unceremoniously booted about the board. White has developed his center pawns with tempo and can expect to conduct a swift attack.

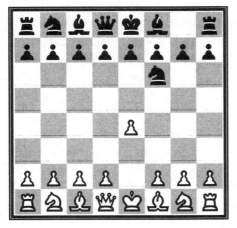

DIAGRAM 71.

3.d4

White calmly occupies the center and opens the diagonals for his Bishops.

There is a great temptation to play 3.c4 Nb6 4.c5 Nd5 5.Bc4 e6 6.Nc3 d6(!), which is called the *Mikenas Variation.* Most top players feel that White has been overzealous in his treatment of the opening and that Black stands with a fair game.

3...d6

The first effects of Black's strategy become apparent: The e-pawn, having been lured forward, is now the object of Black's counterplay. White can take a number of approaches, including 4.Nf3 or 4.Bc4. My preference is for:

4.c4! Nb6   5.exd6

Another popular move, aptly named the *Four Pawns Attack,* is 5.f4, which keeps a broad pawn center. To play either side of the Four Pawns Attack requires a good deal of study because the lines are extremely sharp and one false slip spells disaster.

After White's capture, the position is beginning to take clarity.

5...cxd6

The alternative recapture, 5...exd6, produces a symmetrical pawn structure with White having an easy advantage due to his superior space.

6.Nc3 g6

The best chance for the f8-Bishop to have a life is to fianchetto itself.

7.Be3 Bg7   8.c5!

The first eight moves of the Alekhine Defense are shown in Diagram 72. White expects the following moves, with an advantage to White.

8...dxc5   9.dxc5 N6d7
10.Bc4

Scandinavian Defense

Having journeyed through the classical openings, you might consider the Alekhine Defense to be a bit rash. As I became a stronger player, I was surprised to discover that my old favorite was an accepted defense called the *Scandinavian Defense.*

1.e4 d5!?

DIAGRAM 72.

Black attacks White's e4-pawn and forces a reaction.

2.exd5

This capture is practically forced.

2...Qxd5

This premature developing of the Queen has at least momentarily done its job. White's e4-pawn has disappeared.

Black has also tried 2...Nf6 to recover the pawn without developing the Queen. White can then try 3.Bb5+, 3.c4, or the preferred 3.d4 Nxd5 4.c4 Nb6 5.Nc3, with play as in the Alekhine Defense.

3.Nc3 Qa5

Black tries to get his Queen out of danger. The retreats 3...Qd6 and 3...Qd8 have also been tried, but preference has been shown for the text.

4.d4 Nf6	**5.Nf3 Bg4**
6.h3 Bxf3	**7.Qxf3 c6**

As shown in Diagram 73, White has the advantage of the two Bishops but Black has a surprisingly solid position. The Scandinavian Defense is still played by grandmasters who seek to avoid studying the opening theory necessary for top-level chess. The Scandinavian Defense is a good way of avoiding an adversary's preparation.

DIAGRAM 73.

French Defense

The *French Defense* was an early favorite of mine and one I still play today as a grandmaster. The Alekhine and Scandinavian Defenses don't properly prepare an assault on White's e4-pawn, but the French Defense seeks to prepare the move ...d7-d5. It is distinguished after:

1.e4 e6	**2.d4 d5**

Black attacks the e4-pawn with his d5-pawn, which has been supported by the e6-pawn. White has three major choices about what he wants to do with his e4-pawn. He can trade it, support it, or push it:

- 3.exd5 exd5 (Exchange Variation)
- 3.Nc3
- 3.Nd2 (Tarrasch Variation)
- 3.e5 (Advance Variation, or Nimzovitch Variation)

Each of these choices has a large body of opening theory behind it to support its use. The French Defense is a wonderfully intriguing defense that shows no signs of being exhausted.

Exchange Variation

Quite obviously the moves by Black (1.e4 e6 2.d4 d5) represent a counter-attack in the center. If White decides that he wants to avoid some of the sharp lines listed below, he can opt for a small advantage by playing the *Exchange Variation:*

3.exd5 exd5

Diagram 74 shows the effects of White's pawn trade. The pawn structure is completely symmetrical and White's only advantage is having the right to move. However, being on the move means that White can complete his development just a bit faster than Black and therefore gain a small advantage.

4.Bd3

This violates the principle of developing Knights before Bishops. The idea behind this principle is that the development of the Bishops should be delayed because the pawn structure

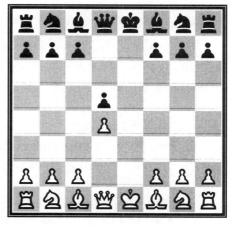

DIAGRAM 74.

in most openings is dynamic. That is, a closed diagonal at one moment suddenly opens. In the French Exchange Variation this is not the case. The pawn structure is well defined. By the text, White develops and tries to prevent ...Bc8-f5, when the Black Bishop develops to a good diagonal.

4...Bd6	5.Nf3 Nf6
6.O-O O-O	7.Bg5 Bg4
8.Nbd2 Nbd7	9.c3 c6
10.Qc2 Qc7	

Both players have completed their development and the game is almost completely equal. Because White has the extra move in a symmetrical position, he has a small plus.

French Defense, 3.Nc3 Variations

By far the most popular way to meet the French Defense (1.e4 e6 2.d4 d5) is with:

3.Nc3

White develops a Knight and protects his e4-pawn. Black has four main moves:

- ■ 3...dxe4 (Rubinstein Variation)
- ■ 3...Bb4 (Winawer Variation)
- ■ 3...Nf6 (Classical or Steinitz Variation)
- ■ 3...Be7 (Seirawan Variation)

Once more, all of these choices are fascinating lines leading to positions that are rich in strategy and tactics.

Rubinstein Variation

One of Black's most consequent decisions in the 3.Nc3 French Defense (1.e4 e6 2.d4 d5 3.Nc3) is to employ the *Rubinstein Variation:*

3...dxe4

Black sought the elimination of the e4-pawn and has now achieved that goal. While White will enjoy a greater freedom of movement for his pieces, Black will aim to trade pieces for a solid position:

4.Nxe4 Nd7   5.Nf3 Ngf6
6.Nxf6+ Nxf6   7.Bd3 Be7
8.Qe2

DIAGRAM 75.

Diagram 75 shows one of the key positions of the Rubinstein Variation. White has the superior Bishops and greater flexibility with his King position. He may castle on either side of the board. Black will aim to play ...c7-c5, neutralizing White's remaining center pawn and solve the problem of his c8-Bishop either by a fianchetto or by playing ...Bc8-d7-c6. Opening theorists believe that White has a slight advantage.

Winawer Variation

Today most French Defense players prefer to play the *Winawer Variation* (1.e4 e6 2.d4 d5 3.Nc3):

3...Bb4

Black pins the Knight and threatens to capture the e-pawn. In most variations of the Winawer, Black will trade his Bishop for the c3-Knight and double White's Queenside pawns. The strategic plans for both sides require study and experience.

4.e5

White advances in the center to grab as much space as he can.

He can also play 4.exd5 exd5, transposing into an Exchange French with Black having committed his Bishop to the b4-square.

Diagram 76, on the next page, shows the main position of the Winawer Variation.

4...c5

DIAGRAM 76.

Black now attacks White's center, hoping to follow up with ...Nb8-c6 to eliminate the central pawns.

5.a3 Bxc3+   6.bxc3

White has strengthened his d4-pawn for the moment, but his doubled Queenside pawns will offer Black counterchances.

6...Ne7

Black initiates a long-term plan to harass the d4-pawn with ...Ne7-f5 in the future.

7.Nf3

This is White's most common move, called the *Rauzer Variation*. White has several other choices:

- ■ 7.a4 is a usual theme. White intends to play a future Bc1-a3, activating his Bishop on a promising diagonal.

- ■ 7.h4 is an amusing echo reaction on the other side of the board! White would like to advance his h-pawn to the h6-square so that he can infiltrate on the weakened dark squares.

- ■ 7.Qg4 is a highly popular Queen sally. White goes on a Kingside raid believing such an adventure is justified due to his control over the center. A sharp reaction by Black is 7...Qc7 8.Qxg7 Rg8 9.Qxh7 cxd4 10.Ne2 Nbc6 11.f4 Bd7 12.Qd3. Black has sacrificed a pawn for the superior development and an exposed White King. Theorists will argue the soundness of Black's sacrifice well into the next millennium. Have fun!

7...Nbc6

In the Rauzer Variation, battle lines are drawn on opposite wings. Usually Black's King is too vulnerable on the Kingside and he is forced to castle Queenside while White's King goes Kingside. A favored line continues:

8.a4 Qa5	9.Bd2 Bd7
10.Bd3 c4	11.Be2 O-O-O
12.O-O	

With a fighting game ahead, practice has favored White.

Steinitz Variation

Most grandmasters prefer to hoard their Bishops, hoping that as the opening moves unfold and the position is opened, their Bishops will powerfully rake the open diagonals. While the Winawer Variation means parting with the f8-Bishop, the *Steinitz Variation* holds onto the Bishop and intensifies the pressure on the e4-pawn (1.e4 e6 2.d4 d5 3.Nc3):

3...Nf6

White usually reacts by gaining a tempo while attacking Black's Knight:

4.e5

Classical Variation

An important strategic alternative for White is (1.e4 e6 2.d4 d5 3.Nc3 Nf6):

4.Bg5

In the French Defense, White usually has difficulties activating his c1-Bishop due to his central d4- and e5-pawns. The idea of this move is to exchange dark-squared Bishops. Play proceeds:

4...Be7	5.e5 Nfd7
6.Bxe7	

White can play an interesting gambit, 6.h4!?, called the *Chatard-Alekhine Attack*.

6...Qxe7	7.f4

White reinforces his e5-pawn and prepares a future f4-f5 break.

7...a6

Black wants to play ...c7-c5, but first wants to prevent Nc3-b5 invading the d6-square.

8.Nf3 c5	9.dxc5 Nxc5
10.Bd3 Nc6	

DIAGRAM 77.

Diagram 77 shows this classical position of the French Defense, with a small advantage for White.

Steinitz Variation, continued

In the Steinitz Variation (1.e4 e6 2.d4 d5 3.Nc3 Nf6 4.e5), White doesn't exchange Bishops, reasoning that Black's Queen will be developed to the good e7-square and keeps the Bishops on the board.

  4...Nfd7   **5.f4**

Just as in the Classical Variation, White reinforces his center.

  5...c5

Now that the f8-Bishop covers the d6-square, Black isn't required to play ...a7-a6 to prevent Nc3-b5, and attacks White's center at once.

  6.Nf3 Nc6 **7.Be3 cxd4**
  8.Nxd4 Bc5

Both players are developing with an aim for central control.

  9.Qd2

Diagram 78 shows the thematic position of the Steinitz Variation. Play often proceeds:

  9...Nxd4 **10.Bxd4 Bxd4**
  11.Qxd4 Qb6 **12.Qxb6 Nxb6**
  13.Nb5 Ke7

This line provides an advantage for White.

DIAGRAM 78.

Seirawan Variation

A relatively modern defensive twist is a variation that I have devised and championed (1.e4 e6 2.d4 d5 3.Nc3):

3...Be7

Although this appears to be a strange move, it is in fact a high-class waiting move. If White plays 4.Nf3 Nf6 5.e5 Nfd7, play has transposed into a Steinitz Variation where White has committed his f3-Knight and has denied himself the opportunity for f2-f4.

If White advances his e-pawn with 4.e5, the advance doesn't come with tempo. Black can now play for the strategically desirable plan of trading light-squared Bishops with 4...b6. Black plays for ...Bc8-a6 with a Bishop trade in sight. White attacks the g7-pawn with 5.Qg4 and hopes to cause some dark-squared weaknesses in Black's camp. Continuing with 5...g6 6.h4 h5! 7.Qf4 Ba6, Black has solved his "problem Bishop" in the French and can face the future with confidence.

White's best test of the *Seirawan Variation* is:

4.Bd3!

This provokes:

4...dxe4   5.Nxe4 Nd7

6.Nf3 Ngf6

Play now transposes into the Rubinstein Variation. I've played this position in provocative style as Black on several occasions:

7.Nxf6+ Bxf6   8.Qe2 c5

9.d5 Nb6   10.Bb5+ Kf8

Diagram 79 shows a crucial position in my variation. My personal tournament score is quite favorable with Black, but the position requires careful study!

DIAGRAM 79.

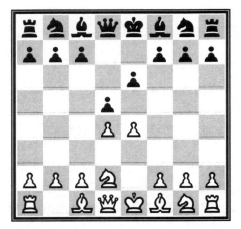

DIAGRAM 80.

Tarrasch Variation

As you've seen from the 3.Nc3 variations, committing the b1-Knight to the c3-square invites a pin and makes it awkward for White to defend the d4-pawn after ...c7-c5. With this in mind, White has taken another approach to the French Defense (1.e4 e6 2.d4 d5):

3.Nd2

White defends his e4-pawn while keeping a flexible approach toward the defense of his center.

Diagram 80 shows the *Tarrasch Variation.* At first glance, the move makes a poor impression because it blocks the c1-Bishop from developing. Black can use this temporary central blocking move to attack White's center; 3...c5 and 3...Nf6 are the principle tries.

3...c5

This is quite a sensible reaction. Black plays to wipe out White's central pawns.

4.exd5

White decides to trade pawns. White gains nothing from 4.c3?! cxd4 5.cxd4 dxe4 6.Nxe4 Bb4+ 7.Nc3 Nf6, which makes an easy game for Black.

4...exd5	**5.Ngf3 Nc6**
6.Bb5 Bd6	**7.O-O Nge7**
8.dxc5 Bxc5	**9.Nb3 Bd6**

At the current position, shown in Diagram 81, White is considered to have a small advantage due to Black's *isolated Queen pawn (IQP)*. The d5-pawn is considered to be weak as it cannot be protected by a fellow pawn and therefore requires the protection of a piece.

If Black prefers a game with more of a French Defense flavor, then the following is the ticket (1.e4 e6 2.d4 d5 3.Nd2):

3...Nf6

White's e-pawn is lured forward.

4.e5 Nfd7   5.f4

In a thematic move that we've seen before, White takes as big a bite of the center as he can swallow.

5...c5   6.c3

This is the key advantage of the Tarrasch Variation. White is able to fortify his center.

6...Nc6   7.Ndf3 cxd4
8.cxd4 Nb6

DIAGRAM 81.

Diagram 82 shows the *Leningrad Variation*. Black focuses his play on the Queenside and White focuses on the Kingside. Opening theory favors White due to his central grip.

Tarrasch–Seirawan Variation

If either of the above lines don't appeal against the Tarrasch Variation, Black can always play: (1.e4 e6 2.d4 d5 3.Nd2) 3...dxe4, transposing into the Rubinstein Variation, or he can wait for White to commit himself:

3...Be7   4.Bd3 dxe4
5.Nxe4 Nd7   6.Nf3 Ngf6

The game has transposed right back into the Rubinstein Variation. (See page 107.)

DIAGRAM 82.

DIAGRAM 83.

Alternatively, White can play (1.e4 e6 2.d4 d5 3.Nd2 Be7):

4.Ngf3 Nf6 **5.e5 Nfd7**
6.Bd3 c5 **7.c3 cxd4**
8.cxd4 b6

As shown in Diagram 83, Black is once again trying to exchange light-squared Bishops and White has been denied the chance for f2-f4.

9.Qe2 a5!

Black pursues his idea of trading Bishops. White has an advantage due to his central pawns, but the Bishop trade will give Black excellent chances to equalize. The Seirawan Variation nicely solves problems in both the 3.Nc3 and Tarrasch Variations of the French Defense.

Advance Variation

White can cut across the earlier opening theory by advancing his e-pawn on move three (1.e4 e6 2.d4 d5):

3.e5

This advance was popularized by Aaron Nimzovitch (1886–1935) who brought many new ideas to this move. Thus the *Advance Variation* often bears his name.

Diagram 84 shows how White grabs as much space in the center as he can and hopes to build up an attack behind the broad shoulders of his central pawns. There is, however,

DIAGRAM 84.

a clear drawback to this advance: It doesn't come with tempo. This means that Black can create a quick counterattack in the center.

3...c5

Black tries to undermine the d4-pawn, which supports the e5-pawn. Black can also play the thematic move 3...b6, again trying to trade Bishops. Most French Defense players prefer to attack the d4-pawn.

Naturally, White plays to keep his d4-pawn intact:

4.c3 Nc6   5.Nf3 Qb6

Black does his best to increase the pressure on the d4-pawn. He has in view a plan of ...Ng8-h6-f5, causing the d-pawn to tremble.

6.Be2

White plays to quickly castle. White has also tried 6.Bd3 and 6.a3, which intends b2-b4 and a Queenside expansion.

6...cxd4   7.cxd4 Nge7
8.Na3 Nf5   9.Nc2

Diagram 85 shows a crucial position of the Advance French. White tries to keep his d4-pawn secure while Black nibbles around the flanks. White has a small advantage.

Caro-Kann Defense

In the Scandinavian and French Defenses, Black attacks the e4-pawn with his d5-pawn. The drawback to the Scandinavian is that the Queen is brought out too quickly, whereas in the French Defense, Black suffers from a cramped c8-Bishop. The *Caro-Kann Defense* intends to attack the e4-pawn without these disadvantages.

1.e4 c6

DIAGRAM 85.

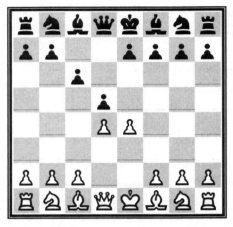

DIAGRAM 86.

Black gives his d-pawn added support in advance.

2.d4 d5

These moves distinguish the Caro-Kann, as shown in Diagram 86.

The Caro-Kann has been embraced by Mikhail Botvinnik (1911–95, World Champion 1948–57, 1958–60, 1961–63) and Anatoly Karpov (1951–, World Champion 1975–85). Every defense has *some* type of a drawback; the Caro-Kann is not appreciated by the b8-Knight because its best square, c6, has been denied. Well, you can't have everything! White has three main tries versus the Caro-Kann Defense:

- 3.Nc3 (Classical Variation)
- 3.exd5 (Exchange Variation)
- 3.e5 (Advance Variation)

Classical Variation

As you've seen from the French Defense, White often defends his e4-pawn (1.e4 c6 2.d4 d5):

3.Nc3 dxe4   4.Nxe4 Bf5

This move shows the advantage of the Caro-Kann Defense. The position is similar to a Rubinstein French Variation but the c8-Bishop emerges at once.

The favored move of Anatoly Karpov is 4...Nd7. Black intends to attack the e4-Knight with one of his own. This is an extremely solid choice. White players have chosen a variety of methods to gain an advantage, and it hasn't been easy. Currently, the favored method is 5.Ng5!? Ngf6 6.Bd3 e6 7.N1f3 Bd6 8.Qe2 h6 9.Ne4 Nxe4 10.Qxe4. The position is shown in Diagram 87.

Theory considers that White has a small advantage after 10...Nf6 11.Qe2 b6 12.Bd2 Bb7 13.0-0-0, when White has the superior development.

5.Ng3

Although White's Knight has been forced to retreat, it does so with tempo.

5...Bg6

Black's Bishop takes up a powerful defensive position on the Kingside. The g6-Bishop is so strong that it is

DIAGRAM 87.

virtually impossible for White to create any meaningful Kingside attacking chances. White's best plan is to try to undermine the Kingside and trade Bishops:

6.h4! h6	**7.Nf3 Nd7**
8.h5 Bh7	**9.Bd3 Bxd3**
10.Qxd3 e6	

Diagram 88 shows the main line of the classical Caro-Kann. White has achieved an advantage in space and development. Black has a solid formation and he will endeavor to catch up in development.

Exchange Variation

If White wants to play a more open game, the *Exchange Variation* is the ticket (1.e4 c6 2.d4 d5):

3.exd5 cxd5

DIAGRAM 88.

117

DIAGRAM 89.

These moves, shown in Diagram 89, open the game a bit. White hopes that having an extra move will give him an advantage. Black is happy to trade away his c6-pawn for White's e4-pawn. White has to make a choice of whether to play c2-c4, attacking the d5-pawn, or whether he would prefer c2-c3 and a quiet existence.

Exchange Variation, Rubinstein Variation

Once more we have an opening variation credited to Akiba Rubinstein (1.e4 c6 2.d4 d5 3.exd5 cxd5):

4.Bd3

White intends to continue with c2-c3 and aim his pieces toward the center and Kingside. This move stops Black's c8-Bishop from developing comfortably.

4...Nc6	5.c3 Nf6

6.Bf4

Diagram 90 shows the position of the Caro-Kann, *Rubinstein Variation*. White's Bishops have taken up wonderful diagonals and Black will have to neutralize them.

6...Bg4

Black wants a solid central formation with his pawn on e6, but he first develops his Bishop before moving his e-pawn.

7.Qb3

DIAGRAM 90.

White can acquiesce to a pinned Knight with 7.Nf3, but he wants to harass the b7-pawn.

> **7...Qd7   8.Nd2 e6**
> **9.Ngf3**

The position is quite balanced. White has a temporary initiative due to his superior mobilization, but Black's position is solid and he can face the future with confidence.

Exchange Variation, Panov-Botvinnik Attack

As an alternative to this quiet line, White can stir up a much sharper game by immediately attacking Black's d5-pawn (1.e4 c6 2.d4 d5 3.exd5 cxd5):

> **4.c4**

White hopes to use his extra starting move to gain an advantage. This follow-up, called the *Panov-Botvinnik Attack,* requires a cautious approach on Black's part.

> **4...Nf6   5.Nc3**

The careful reader will note a remarkable similarity between this position and the Tarrasch Defense to the Queen's Gambit. (See Diagram 63.) The only difference is that White now has an extra move! If Black were to play 5...g6, it would be like a Schlechter Variation with reversed colors.

Black usually chooses to reinforce his d5-pawn:

> **5...e6   6.Nf3 Be7**

Black quickly develops to bring his King to safety.

> **7.cxd5 Nxd5   8.Bd3 O-O**
> **9.O-O**

The key position of the Panov-Botvinnik Attack is shown in Diagram 91. White has accepted an isolated Queen pawn that will need support,

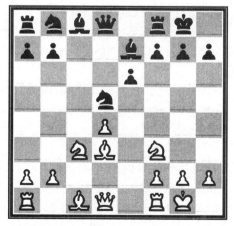

DIAGRAM 91.

DIAGRAM 92.

and he hopes to utilize his space and superior development to gain a King-side attack. After decades of practice, White has been able to show a small plus.

Advance Variation

If White isn't satisfied with defending his e4-pawn or trading it for the d5-pawn, he can advance his pawn (1.e4 c6 2.d4 d5):

> **3.e5**

As shown in Diagram 92, White has grabbed space as in the French Defense, Advance Variation and is pleased to see Black's pawn on the c6-square where it doesn't attack his d4-pawn. But if the Caro-Kann Defense, *Advance Variation* has a drawback, it is that Black can develop his c8-Bishop outside of his central pawn chain:

> **3...Bf5**

White must now make a decision. Should he seek to attack the f5-Bishop with g2-g4? Should he trade the Bishop with a Bf1-d3? Or should he ignore the f5-Bishop altogether?

These are interesting questions and I'll look at four possibilities: 4.g4, 4.Nc3, 4.h4 and 4.Nf3.

Advance Variation, Flank Attack

The Advance Variation (1.e4 c6 2.d4 d5 3.e5 Bf5) can provoke a radical solution. White decides upon a quick attack on the flank:

> **4.g4(?!)**

This questionable move still has its supporters. White hopes to gain time and space on the Kingside by attacking the f5-Bishop.

> **4...Be4!**

Black provokes White to advance his f-pawn.

5.f3 Bg6   **6.h4**

White tries to further disturb the Bishop and make the Kingside the theater of battle.

White has also tried 6.e6?! Qd6!, when Black has the superior game.

Black must stop White's threat of h4-h5 winning the Bishop.

6...h5   **7.Nh3 e6!**

8.Nf4 hxg4   **9.Nxg6 fxg6**

Diagram 93 shows White's Kingside attack to be in shambles.

10.fxg4 Rxh4

White is a pawn down and Black has the initiative.

DIAGRAM 93.

Advance Variation, Flank Attack

As you've just seen, if White is set upon a flank expansion he should prepare it (1.e4 c6 2.d4 d5 3.e5 Bf5):

4.Nc3

White protects the e4-square so that Black is denied the chance for ...Bf5-e4.

4...e6   **5.g4 Bg6**

6.Nge2

The position shown in Diagram 94 has led to fascinating games. Grandmasters Jan Timman and John Nunn, two of the most aggressive players on the circuit, like White's position. Black has tried 6...Qh4,

DIAGRAM 94.

thereby preventing h2-h4 and trying to weaken the Kingside. It is usual to counterattack in the center:

6...c5   7.h4 h6

Black has also tried 7...h5 8.Nf4 with a sharp game.

8.Be3 Nc6   9.f4 Qb6

With a dynamic position, both players have winning chances.

Advance Variation, Flank Attack

An interesting twist on the Advance Variation, Flank Attack (1.e4 c6 2.d4 d5 3.e5 Bf5) is this preparatory move:

4.h4

This cunning move is favored by Boris Spassky. Black must avoid playing 4...e6?? 5.g4 Be4 6.f3 Bg6 7.h5, when Black loses his Bishop .

4...h5

Black reacts with a necessary defensive move. Weaker is 4...h6 5.g4 Bd7 6.h5!, with advantage to White; or 4...h6 5.g4 Bh7 6.e6! fxe6 7.Bd3!, with a promising attack for the sacrificed pawn.

The drawback of 4...h5 is that the g5-square now falls into White's mitt.

5.c4 e6   6.Nc3 Ne7

7.Nf3 Nd7

White's trump is the g5-square and Black's is the f5-square. Both players will use these squares to aggressively post their minor pieces. The chances are roughly equal.

Advance Variation, Short Variation

One of the most imaginative ways of meeting the Caro-Kann Defense has been championed by the British grandmaster Nigel Short. His idea in the Advance Variation (1.e4 c6 2.d4 d5 3.e5 Bf5) is to allow Black's f5-Bishop to "peacefully co-exist." In other words, ignore what Black has done and get on with controlling space in the center:

4.Nf3

This is a radical departure from the other lines in the Advance Variation. It was always considered necessary to harass the f5-Bishop as quickly as possible, lest Black get an easy game.

4...e6   5.Be2

White's last two moves really distinguish the *Caro-Kann Advance, Short Variation*. (See Diagram 95.) White quietly completes his development and leaves it up to Black to construct a central counter.

DIAGRAM 95.

5...c5   6.O-O

One of the benefits of Short's variation is that the f5-Bishop is often vulnerable on its square to a Nf3xd4 recapture.

6...Ne7

Black has to be careful that his Knights don't trip over one another. For instance, after 6...Nc6 7.c3 cxd4 8.cxd4 Nge7 9.Be3, Black's Kingside pieces are entangled. Black envisions ...Ne7-c6 so that the b8-Knight can go to the d7-square.

7.dxc5

White can consider 7.c3, 7.c4 and 7.Nbd2 as reasonable alternatives.

7...Nec6   8.a3 Bxc5
9.b4 Be7   10.c4

White enjoys more space and Black has good piece play. The position is approximately equal.

Sicilian Defense

Of the modern defenses to a King Pawn Opening, the overwhelming favorite is the Sicilian Defense:

DIAGRAM 96.

1.e4 c5

This is the granddaddy of modern defenses. The plans are so rich and varied for both sides that hundreds of books have been written about this provocative and complex defense. In an effort not to overwhelm the poor reader, I'll just tread lightly upon the major defenses.

As shown in Diagram 96, Black hasn't tried to block White's e4-pawn with ...e7-e5, nor has he tried to attack the e4-pawn with ...Ng8-f6 or ...d7-d5. Instead, Black has left the e4-pawn alone and has struck out on his own scheme. For the moment, Black controls the d4-square.

In viewing Diagram 96, the Classicist would condemn Black's move because unlike White's move, Black's move doesn't support the development of a Bishop. Infatuated by quick development, it is easy to overlook that Black is using a flank pawn to control the center. His own e- and d-pawns stay behind, awaiting instructions. This is the key to understanding the Sicilian structures: Black isn't interested in *occupying the center,* he wants to *control the center from a distance.*

From Diagram 96, White has two options: either play for d2-d4, called the *Open Sicilian;* or do not play for d2-d4, called the *Closed Sicilian.* The current survey focuses upon Open Sicilian positions.

White has several ways of playing for d2-d4. He can do it at once, or he can support the advance with the moves c2-c3 or Ng1-f3.

Smith-Morra Gambit

In the first scenario, White doesn't waste any time in achieving the desired move. He simply occupies the center (1.e4 c5).

2.d4 cxd4

Naturally, Black isn't about to let White keep a classical center. Now White must decide how to recapture the d4-pawn. If he plays 3.Qxd4? Nc6, his Queen is lured into the center prematurely, and Black has superior play. He can play 3.Nf3, anticipating Nf3xd4, which will transpose into a variation described later in this chapter. Instead White initiates the *Smith-Morra Gambit:*

3.c3

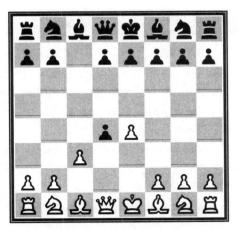

DIAGRAM 97.

Diagram 97 shows the current position. Just as in the Danish Gambit, White offers a pawn for quick development.

Smith-Morra Gambit Declined

Black can decline the gambit by:

3...d5	**4.exd5 Qxd5**
5.cxd4 Nf6	**6.Nc3 Qd8**

The position is another famous isolated Queen pawn position, which often transposes from a Panov-Botvinnik Attack in the Caro-Kann Defense. Each IQP position must be looked at specifically. In this case, Black has all the usual advantages and disadvantages, no more or less.

Smith-Morra Gambit Accepted

Opening theory books rightfully question the soundness of the Smith-Morra Gambit (1.e4 c5 2.d4 cxd4 3.c3).

3...dxc3	**4.Nxc3**

Black should accept the sacrifice and force White to show compensation for the pawn. The problem is that while theory is dry and scientific, facing the Smith-Morra Gambit in over-the-board play is tough! Beginners usually get slammed by the gambit. Black has to play very cautiously indeed!

4...e6

Black uses this important move to close the a2-g8 diagonal (something he can't do in the Danish Gambit), which makes his defense much easier. This move also takes away the d5-square for White's c3-Knight.

5.Nf3 Nc6   6.Bc4

White tries to bring his pieces to their most active squares. Although the a2-g8 diagonal is closed, the Bishop has no better prospects elsewhere.

6...a6

Black spends a whole tempo to defend the b5-square. This dangerous loss of time precludes White's c3-Knight from a potential jump to the d6-square.

7.O-O Qc7

I know that it is hard to believe that Black should be moving his Queen so early, but he wants to avoid 7...Nf6 8.Bg5, when his Knight is pinned.

8.Qe2

Diagram 98 shows the impressive lead in development that White has achieved. However, Black hasn't created any real targets for White to grasp and Black shows he has kept a flexible and solid position.

DIAGRAM 98.

8...Nf6   9.Bg5 Ng4
10.Rad1

White had to prevent ...Nc6-d4, which would strip White's defender of the h2-pawn.

10...d6

Black controls the e5-square and has the slightly better chances. Even so, White's position is very dangerous to the average amateur player!

Alapin Variation

A great amount of theory exists on the Sicilian Defense, which leads many players to seek refuge in the *Alapin Variation* (1.e4 c5):

2.c3

The Alapin, shown in Diagram 99, has the noble aim of establishing a classical pawn center, but it is really rather harmless.

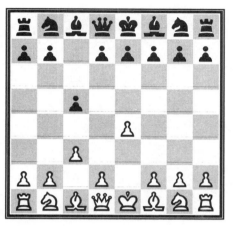

2...d5	**3.exd5 Qxd5**
4.d4 cxd4	**5.cxd4 Nf6**
6.Nc3 Qd8	

DIAGRAM 99.

The exact same position is reached as in the Smith-Morra Gambit Declined discussed earlier. Black can try to improve on this isolated Queen pawn position by trying (1.e4 c5 2.c3 d5 3.exd5 Qxd5 4.d4) 4...Nf6 5.Nf3 Bg4 6.Be2 e6. In either case, White cannot expect much of an advantage.

Open Sicilian, Main Line

In his quest to conquer the center, White realizes that he will need to play d2-d4. As the prelude to an Open Sicilian, he decides to utilize his g1-Knight (1.e4 c5):

2.Nf3

Black has to decide how he wants to play with his center pawns: 2...d6 or 2...e6. While often transposing, these moves also lead to vastly different formations.

Scheveningen Variation

This variation offers a quintessential example of the Open Sicilian Defense (1.e4 c5 2.Nf3):

2...d6

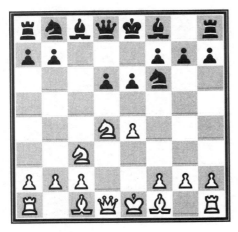

DIAGRAM 100.

Black awaits White's center push.

3.d4

White has also tried 3.Bb5+ Bd7 4.Bxd7+ Qxd7 5.c4, called the *Moscow Variation.* But with this variation, White has traded Bishops and helped Black's development.

3...cxd4   **4.Nxd4**

White's point. He has brought his Knight into the action in the center of the board where it controls many squares.

4...Nf6   **5.Nc3 e6**

Diagram 100 displays the *Scheveningen Variation* of the Sicilian, and it is an excellent position to spend a long time staring at. Ask yourself as many questions from the perspective of the principles as you can. It will be a very useful exercise.

Diagram 100 shows that Black has taken a *restrained* approach to the center. He hasn't tried to *occupy* it, but observe how the d6- and e6-pawns *control* two of the sweet center squares and that the f6-Knight attacks the e4-square. This formation is the favorite of Garry Kasparov, and he used it in many games to become the World Champion!

I urge any player who wants to understand the keys of the Sicilian Defense to start from this position. White has taken a number of approaches to the Scheveningen, including:

- 6.Bc4 (Fischer Attack)
- 6.Be2 (Maroczy Variation)
- 6.g4 (Keres Attack)
- 6.f4 (Tal Variation)

Scheveningen Variation, Fischer Attack

The *Fischer Attack* is a straight-forward concept that begins (1.e4 c5 2.Nf3 d6 3.d4 cxd4 4.Nxd4 Nf6 5.Nc3 e6):

6.Bc4

White tries to clamp down on the d5-square, with an eye toward attacking the e6-pawn with f2-f4-f5. Black has a variety of defenses based upon …Nb8-c6-a5 or …Nb8-d7-c5 in conjunction with …a7-a6 and …b7-b5-b4 going for the e4-pawn. A solid choice is:

6…Be7   7.Bb3 O-O
8.Be3

White prepares to castle Queenside.

8…Na6

Black decides to bring his Knight to the c5-square to eliminate the b3-Bishop. One of the tactics that Black has to be aware of is 8…Nbd7 9.Bxe6!? fxe6 10.Nxe6 Qa5 11.Nxf8 Bxf8, where White sacrifices two pieces for a Rook.

9.Qe2 Nc5   10.f3

Diagram 101 features a common position from the Fischer Attack. White will aim for g2-g4-g5 and a Kingside pawn storm. Black will play …a7-a6 and …b7-b5 for an attack on the Queenside. The position is dynamically balanced.

DIAGRAM 101.

Scheveningen Variation, Maroczy Variation

In the *Maroczy Variation*, White takes a more restrained approach to the center. He first aims to complete his Kingside development, delaying an attack for awhile (1.e4 c5 2.Nf3 d6 3.d4 cxd4 4.Nxd4 Nf6 5.Nc3 e6):

DIAGRAM 102.

**6.Be2 Be7   7.O-O Nc6
8.Kh1**

White tucks his King away to the h1-square. He is committed to playing f2-f4, and wants to avoid tactics based on the g1-a7 diagonal.

8...O-O   9.f4 a6

Black guards the b5-square and prepares the c7-square for his Queen.

10.Be3 Qc7

Diagram 102 shows the Maroczy.

In their 1995 PCA Championship Match, Viswanathan Anand and Garry Kasparov played this position a number of times. The position is dynamically balanced.

Scheveningen Variation, Keres Attack

By far the greatest challenge to the Scheveningen Variation is the *Keres Attack,* which begins (1.e4 c5 2.Nf3 d6 3.d4 cxd4 4.Nxd4 Nf6 5.Nc3 e6):

DIAGRAM 103.

6.g4

As shown in Diagram 103, White immediately starts his Kingside attack in motion. The threat to play g4-g5 and kick the f6-Knight into oblivion is one that theorists have long debated. Should Black allow White to carry out his threat, or play ...h7-h6, creating a weakness? This question produces two distinct variations.

Scheveningen Variation, Keres Attack (without ...h7-h6)

Black can allow White to carry out his threat, as follows (1.e4 c5 2.Nf3 d6 3.d4 cxd4 4.Nxd4 Nf6 5.Nc3 e6 6.g4):

6...Nc6	7.g5 Nd7
8.Be3 a6	9.h4 Qc7
10.f4 b5	

White has extended his Kingside in order to launch an attack, while Black is busily preparing ...Bc8-b7 and ...Nd7-c5 with a counterattack

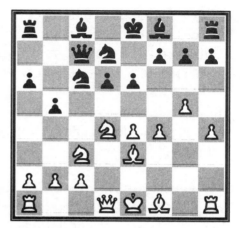

DIAGRAM 104.

against the e4-pawn. The position shown in Diagram 104 is uncommonly sharp, but I prefer White's position.

Scheveningen Variation, Keres Attack (with ...h7-h6)

Scheveningen players by and large prefer to slow down White's expansion by playing (1.e4 c5 2.Nf3 d6 3.d4 cxd4 4.Nxd4 Nf6 5.Nc3 e6 6.g4):

6...h6	7.g5 hxg5
8.Bxg5	

Diagram 105 shows the position, which is extremely difficult to evaluate. Black's h8-Rook has been "developed" without having moved—a certain plus for Black. The trade of a Black h-pawn for a White g-pawn means that neither player is going to castle on the Kingside. Probably both Kings will move Queenside. White's menacing g5-Bishop must be

DIAGRAM 105.

131

carefully observed as the tactics of f2-f4 and e4-e5 will hang over Black's position. A usual continuation would be:

8...Nc6	**9.f4 Be7**
10.Qd2 a6	**11.O-O-O Qc7**
12.h4 Bd7	

This leads to another one of those bottomless Sicilian positions that defy conventional understanding. Theorists have a slight preference for White in this position.

Scheveningen Variation, Tal Variation

Our final look at meeting the Scheveningen Variation of the Sicilian Defense (1.e4 c5 2.Nf3 d6 3.d4 cxd4 4.Nxd4 Nf6 5.Nc3 e6) exhibits a completely different plan by White. Mikhail Tal (1936–92, World Champion 1960–61), a master of the attack, introduced the scheme of a quick Queenside castling:

6.f4

White wants to create immediate central threats with e4-e5. Black has to keep a wary eye to this possibility.

6...Nc6	**7.Be3 Be7**

8.Qf3

Diagram 106 shows Tal's idea. What he wants to do is quickly castle Queenside and reintroduce the threat of e4-e5 after White's Rook is sitting on the d1-square. In many lines, when the players castle on opposite wings, White's Queen is ready to support the charge of the g-pawn. The position is dynamically balanced.

DIAGRAM 106.

Dragon Variation

I started my description of the Open Sicilian Defense with the Scheveningen Variation because that is really the classical way of handling the Sicilian. Black's e6- and d6-pawns act as a central buffer between the two armies. Of course, this central buffer is quite dynamic and Black can try a number of different central structures. A favorite of mine, if only for the name, is the *Dragon Variation*. I covered this defense in

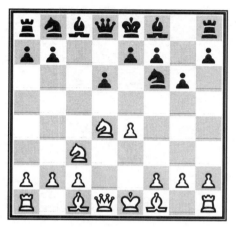

DIAGRAM 107.

some depth in *Winning Chess Brilliancies* (Microsoft Press, 1995), and I urge you to probe there for a deeper understanding of this line.

The Dragon Variation, shown in Diagram 107, is reached after (1.e4 c5 2.Nf3 d6 3.d4 cxd4 4.Nxd4 Nf6 5.Nc3):

5...g6

Note Black's pawn structure: h7-g6-f7-e7-d6, which resembles a dragon. Black goes for a Kingside fianchetto where the g7-Bishop will have a strong influence along the long diagonal. From White's perspective, Black has failed to adequately keep the d5-square guarded, and he can use this point to his advantage. If Black tries a later ...e7-e6, the d6-pawn will be vulnerable. The Dragon can be met in an expected variety of ways that all boil down to a crucial decision: Will White castle Kingside or Queenside? Once White decides where he'd like to park his King, he can decide which formation he likes best.

Dragon Variation (with Kingside Castling), Levenfish Attack

One popular attacking scheme for White is the *Levenfish Attack* (1.e4 c5 2.Nf3 d6 3.d4 cxd4 4.Nxd4 Nf6 5.Nc3 g6):

6.f4

DIAGRAM 108.

White threatens e4-e5, which Black immediately prevents.

> **6...Nc6**　　**7.Nf3 Bg7**
> **8.Bd3 O-O**　　**9.O-O**

Diagram 108 shows a common position of the Levenfish Attack. White's attacking scheme is to play Qd1-e1-h4 in conjunction with f4-f5 and Bc1-h6. Black has to come up with a reaction. If he plays 9...d5? 10.e5!, White will have a big advantage. Thus it is difficult for Black to make a meaningful counter in the center. Black can try to distract White's pieces from the Kingside by playing a line like 9...b6 10.Qe1 Nb4 11.Qh4 Nxd3 12.cxd3 Ba6. Practice has shown the position to be dynamically equal.

Dragon Variation (with Kingside Castling), Nottingham Variation

As an alternative to the Levenfish Attack, White can take a more restrained approach (1.e4 c5 2.Nf3 d6 3.d4 cxd4 4.Nxd4 Nf6 5.Nc3 g6):

> **6.Be2 Bg7**　　**7.Be3 Nc6**
> **8.Nb3**

DIAGRAM 109.

White's last move distinguishes the *Nottingham Variation.* (See Diagram 109.) White's approach is to keep the d5-square firmly in his sights.

> **8...O-O**　　**9.O-O**

White intends to keep the center well patrolled by playing f2-f4 and Be2-f3. Black's space deficit encourages him to trade pieces and a common line is:

9...Be6

This is possible now that White's d4-Knight has retreated.

10.f4 Na5

Black's point is revealed; he is playing to put a piece on the c4-square:

11.f5 Bc4

This final position is known as the *Byrne Variation*. White has a slight advantage as he tries to stir up trouble on the Kingside.

Dragon Variation (with Queenside Castling), Yugoslav Attack

While castling Kingside by White can certainly bring about attacking schemes, the sharpest lines of the Dragon Variation occur when White castles Queenside (1.e4 c5 2.Nf3 d6 3.d4 cxd4 4.Nxd4 Nf6 5.Nc3 g6):

6.Be3

White quickly develops his Queenside pieces in order to make way for castling.

6...Bg7

A painful trap would be 6...Ng4?? 7.Bb5+! Bd7 8.Qxg4.

7.f3

White rules out a possible ...Nf6-g4, which would disrupt his development.

7...O-O   8.Qd2 Nc6

Diagram 110 shows a critical position in the Dragon Sicilian. White has prepared to castle long but he is concerned about a possible ...d6-d5 and decides to clamp down on the d5-square.

9.Bc4 Bd7   10.O-O-O Rc8

11.Bb3

DIAGRAM 110.

135

The battle lines have been drawn. With Kings on opposite wings, it is a given that both armies will go after the other's monarch. White usually plays for h2-h4-h5 in conjunction with Be3-h6 to weaken Black's King. Black usually plays for …Nc6-e5-c4 to block the b3-Bishop and force trades. Black's counterplay is centered down the c-file. This position is known as the *Yugoslav Attack* and has provided a bounty of beautiful attacking games. The position is dynamically balanced.

Najdorf Variation

Arguably the most complex Sicilian formation of all is the *Najdorf Variation*, which begins with a move of great cunning (1.e4 c5 2.Nf3 d6 3.d4 cxd4 4.Nxd4 Nf6 5.Nc3):

5…a6

Diagram 111 shows the starting position of the Najdorf Variation. As we've seen in the Scheveningen Variation and the Smith-Morra Gambit Accepted, the move …a7-a6 is quite useful. Black controls the b5-square and makes the plan of …b7-b5 and …Bc8-b7 a possibility. Before going into the many approaches that White can try, the move 5…a6 deserves a reproach. The move does nothing to control the sweet center, which is a violation of our cherished principles. White is given free rein over play in the center. Despite the doubts raised, White's ability to get a grip on the position is quite elusive. At times the central pawn buffer can radically change. Black might play …e7-e6 or …e7-e5, requiring White to change his plans. The following is a *short* list of White's approaches:

DIAGRAM 111.

■ 6.Bc4, 6.Be2, 6.g3, and 6.h3 are all based upon the

theme of developing White's f1-Bishop. The latter is a humorous echo of Black's "wasted" tempo on the Queenside. If Black wants to expand on the wing with ...b7-b5, White will expand on the Kingside with g2-g4 and Bf1-g2 for a position similar to a Keres Attack.

- 6.Bg5 and 6.Be3 lines are based upon the idea of clearing the Queenside quickly so that White can castle there.

- 6.a4 is a positional approach to the Queenside. White rules out ...b7-b5 and sometimes plays a4-a5 to clamp down on the b6-square.

- 6.f4 introduces the threat of e4-e5 and grabs a larger share of the center. After 6...e6 7.Qf3, White plays as in the Tal Variation of the Scheveningen.

All of these plans are so complex and varied that separate books have been written about them. In fact, many books have been written on variations further down the chain of moves! With apologies to my readers, I'll take a look only at the greatest test facing the Najdorf:

6.Bg5

Choosing the most dynamic move, White develops a piece and begins a hand-to-hand struggle with the f6-Knight. Black's position is under immediate pressure.

6...e6

Black's Queen now protects the f6-Knight and prevents White from doubling the Kingside pawns.

7.f4

In another fine strengthening move, White introduces the threat of e4-e5 and f4-f5.

This position is literally *the starting position* for most Najdorf players. White's threat of e4-e5 must be addressed. I'll examine each of these moves that Black has played:

- 7...Nbd7

- 7...Qc7
- 7...Qb6 (Poisoned Pawn Variation)
- 7...b5 (Polugaevsky Variation)
- 7...Be7 (the main line)

7...Nbd7

Although it's not that popular, this move makes sense. Black covers the e5-square and reinforces the f6-Knight. The drawback to this move is that the e6-pawn can be quickly attacked:

8.Bc4 b5   9.Bxe6 fxe6

10.Nxe6 Qa5

This piece sacrifice is shown in Diagram 112. In theory, Black is supposed to be all right, but not too many players are anxious to play Black's position.

Our next line is an interesting offbeat idea (1.e4 c5 2.Nf3 d6 3.d4 cxd4 4.Nxd4 Nf6 5.Nc3 a6 6.Bg5 e6 7.f4):

7...Qc7

Black gets out of the pin, controls the c4-square, thereby preventing the type of sacrifice shown in Diagram 112, and invites White to double his Kingside pawns. Black's play is based on the trick:

8.Bxf6 gxf6   9.Qh5 Qc5!

Black is now able to offer an exchange of Queens. On his ninth move, White can build up pressure on the e6-square by:

9.f5 Nc6   10.Bc4 Nxd4

11.Qxd4 Be7   12.O-O-O Bd7

Diagram 113 shows the position, in which White has an advantage.

DIAGRAM 112.

Najdorf Variation, Poisoned Pawn Variation

One of Bobby Fischer's favorite defensive weapons was the *Poisoned Pawn Variation* of the Najdorf. It comes about after (1.e4 c5 2.Nf3 d6 3.d4 cxd4 4.Nxd4 Nf6 5.Nc3 a6 6.Bg5 e6 7.f4):

7...Qb6

As shown in Diagram 114, Black has no respect for the principles that we have worked so hard to learn. The rascal! The commander of the Black

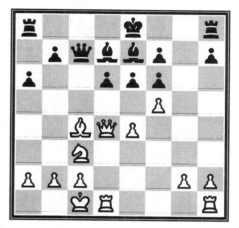

DIAGRAM 113.

pieces is truly a gangster. Not only is he not worried about protecting himself on the Kingside, he brings out his Queen in such a manner as to rob White of his b2-pawn! In principle, Black's play *must be wrong*. But both in theory and practice it is hard to prove it! If anyone finds a refutation to the Poisoned Pawn, please send a letter labeled "top secret" to my post office box. In the main line Poisoned Pawn, White jettisons his b2-pawn for quick development:

8.Qd2

White can also protect the b2-pawn by playing 8.Nb3, but after 8...Qe3+ 9.Qe2 Qxe2+ 10.Bxe2 Nbd7, White's advantage is slight.

8...Qxb2	**9.Rb1 Qa3**	
10.Bxf6 gxf6	**11.f5 Nc6**	

The position shown in Diagram 115, on the next page, has been a source of endless theoretical debate.

DIAGRAM 114.

139

DIAGRAM 115.

Najdorf Variation, Polugaevsky Variation

Yet another vexing continuation of the Sicilian Najdorf is the *Polugaevsky Variation* (1.e4 c5 2.Nf3 d6 3.d4 cxd4 4.Nxd4 Nf6 5.Nc3 a6 6.Bg5 e6 7.f4):

7...b5

Russian grandmaster Lev Polugaevsky devised this monstrous move, shown in Diagram 116.

Black is not oblivious to White's threat of e4-e5; on the contrary, he encourages it. Furthermore, Black shows his intention to start his own counterattack with ...b5-b4, pushing away the nicely placed c3-Knight. What arrogance! White accepts the challenge:

8.e5 dxe5   9.fxe5 Qc7

This is Polugaevsky's point. After 10.exf6 Qe5+ 11.Qe2 Qxg5, Black has traded pieces.

DIAGRAM 116.

10.Qe2 Nfd7   11.O-O-O Nc6!

It would be a mistake to capture the e5-pawn. 11...Qxe5 12.Qxe5 Nxe5 13.Ndxb5 leads to threats of Nb5-c7 and Rd1-d8, with checkmate in both cases. After Black's careful eleventh move the position is dynamically balanced.

Najdorf Variation, Main Line

By now you should be getting an idea of just how complex the Sicilian Najdorf has become. But wait,

we haven't gotten to the main line!
(1.e4 c5 2.Nf3 d6 3.d4 cxd4 4.Nxd4
Nf6 5.Nc3 a6 6.Bg5 e6 7.f4)

7...Be7

This natural developing move is the
most popular way to play the Najdorf. Black breaks the pin and prepares to castle out of the central
dangers.

8.Qf3

White makes way for his own King
to castle.

8...Qc7

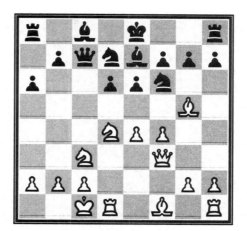

DIAGRAM 117.

Black has also played the Najdorf with 8...h6 9.Bh4, intending to provoke
a sharp encounter by playing ...g7-g5.

9.O-O-O Nbd7

The position shown in Diagram 117 is considered yet another *starting
point* of the Najdorf Sicilian! Theorists have devoted a dozen moves and
more to the best plans for White and Black. I suspect they will still be
debating for centuries to come. It is impossible to say that an "equilibrium" has been established. Both sides have their advantages and I'll just
say the position provides both players with good winning prospects.

Classical Variation

In the Sicilian formations we've looked at so far, Black has delayed the
development of his b8-Knight. When he brings out both of his Knights at
the start of the opening, I consider this to be the *Classical Variation*. Of
course, the positions are highly transpositional as we shall see. Play
begins (1.e4 c5 2.Nf3 d6 3.d4 cxd4 4.Nxd4 Nf6 5.Nc3):

5...Nc6

In *classical style*, Black develops his Knight to its most aggressive square.

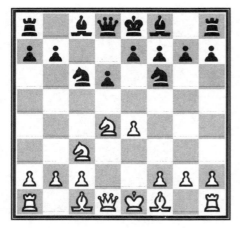

DIAGRAM 118.

Diagram 118 shows the starting position. White must now decide upon his approach. If he plays 6.Be2, Black can play 6...e6, transposing to the Scheveningen, where Black has dodged the Keres Attack. Or Black could play 6...g6, where he has dodged the Yugoslav Attack in the Dragon. Or Black might change the features of the position to an all-together different variety:

6.Be2 e5

Black's sixth move, depicted in Diagram 119, is called the *Boleslavsky Variation*. Black creates a weakness on the d5-square, but he intends to play ...d6-d5 and dissolve the backward d6-pawn. Play might proceed:

7.Nb3 Be6   8.Bg5 Be7

9.O-O O-O

With a puzzling strategic battle ahead, White is considered to have an advantage.

If White is dissatisfied with (1.e4 c5 2.Nf3 d6 3.d4 cxd4 4.Nxd4 Nf6 5.Nc3 Nc6) 6.Be2, he can play 6.Bc4, playing for the Fischer Attack from the Scheveningen Variation. Black loses some flexibility because his b8-Knight has committed itself.

DIAGRAM 119.

Classical Variation, Richter-Rauzer Attack

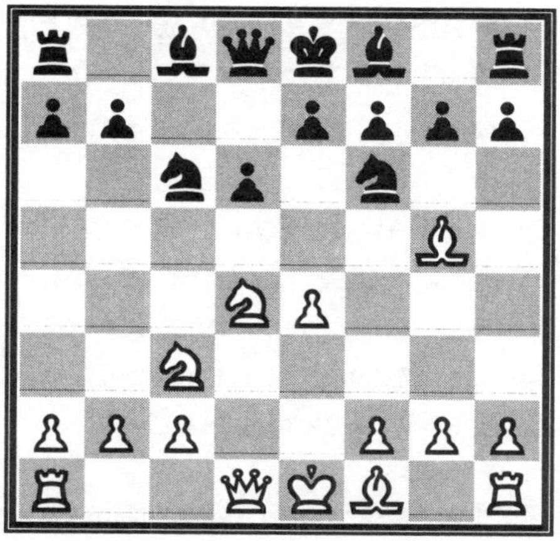

Because of the highly transpositional nature of the Classical Variation, White usually strives to play the forcing *Richter-Rauzer Attack* so that he can override the various transpositions (1.e4 c5 2.Nf3 d6 3.d4 cxd4 4.Nxd4 Nf6 5.Nc3 Nc6):

6.Bg5

The Richter-Rauzer is shown in Diagram 120. White sensibly develops his Bishop as in the Najdorf. For

DIAGRAM 120.

Black, the possibility of playing the Dragon is less desirable. After 6...g6?! 7.Bxf6 exf6, White has damaged Black's pawn structure. The common course is:

6...e6   7.Qd2 Be7

8.O-O-O O-O

A typically sharp Sicilian game is in sight. The classical Sicilian is one of the most popular formations for Black in modern chess. The position provides equal chances for both sides.

Sicilian Defense, 2...e6 Variations

So far our survey has focused upon (1.e4 c5 2.Nf3 d6). Black also has a major choice on move two of playing (1.e4 c5 2.Nf3):

2...e6

This creates an entirely different complex of opening formations. Each has its own peculiarities.

3.d4 cxd4   4.Nxd4

Diagram 121, on the next page, shows the position, with Black having to decide between three main choices:

- 4...a6 (Paulsen Variation)
- 4...Nc6 (Szen Variation)
- 4...Nf6 (Pin Variation)

Paulsen Variation

Of these three choices, the first is the one that gives this line of the Sicilian its unique flavor (1.e4 c5 2.Nf3 e6 3.d4 cxd4 4.Nxd4):

4...a6

Black's fourth move introduces the *Paulsen Variation.* It seems to be a mocking move as Black pays no

DIAGRAM 121.

attention to the sweet center. Instead, he just covers the b5-square and sets up for possible Queenside counterplay. At first it seems that Black has created a weak d6-square, but it is quite difficult for White to land a piece there. Usually, White ignores what Black has done and instead of trying to punish him immediately for his transgressing of our beloved principles, White calmly develops. He has three choices:

- 5.Nc3 (Taimanov Variation)
- 5.c4 (Reti Variation)
- 5.Bd3 (Gipslis Variation)

Paulsen Sicilian, Taimanov Variation

A natural reaction by White is to simply develop the Knight and control the sweet center (1.e4 c5 2.Nf3 e6 3.d4 cxd4 4.Nxd4 a6):

5.Nc3 Qc7

Once more, Black seems to mock the opening principles. He brings out his Queen to control the e5-square and to see how White will commit his forces.

6.Bd3 Nc6   7.Be3 Nf6

144

This is Black's first benefit of his unusual move order. He has avoided Bc1-g5 and the problems that move can cause.

8.O-O Ne5

Black's position is shown in Diagram 122. Russian grandmaster Mark Taimanov introduced this plan for Black, and it now bears his name: the *Taimanov Variation*. Black is looking for an opportunity to play ...Ne5-g4, winning the advantage of two Bishops. At the

DIAGRAM 122.

same time, he has kept the f8-a3 diagonal open so that he can consider ...Bf8-c5, developing the Bishop to a more active square. Black's position in Diagram 122 is a provocative one.

9.h3

White winds up for f2-f4 and e4-e5, with a rout in the center. Once more, the complexities are quite dizzying and the Taimanov Variation remains a favorite in grandmaster play.

Paulsen Sicilian, Reti Variation

One of the ways that White should consider "punishing" Black's move order is by (1.e4 c5 2.Nf3 e6 3.d4 cxd4 4.Nxd4 a6):

5.c4

As shown in Diagram 123, Black has not provoked Nb1-c3 by ...Ng8-f6, and thus White's c2-pawn can stake a claim to the sweet center. This

DIAGRAM 123.

move introduces the *Reti Variation*. White aims to keep both the breaks
...b7-b5 and ...d7-d5 from being played.

5...Nf6   6.Nc3 Bb4

Black exerts pressure on the e4-pawn.

7.Bd3 Nc6   8.Bc2

White has the superior position due to his central control.

Paulsen Sicilian, Gipslis Variation

In this final look at the Paulsen Sicilian, White is also a little crafty with his
move order (1.e4 c5 2.Nf3 e6 3.d4 cxd4 4.Nxd4 a6):

5.Bd3

White supports his e4-pawn and camouflages his intentions. Will he play
for f2-f4 or c2-c4?

5...Nf6   6.O-O

White's threat is to play e4-e5, which Black now prevents:

6...d6   7.c4

White plays in the same manner as in the Reti Variation, but Black's f8-
Bishop isn't active.

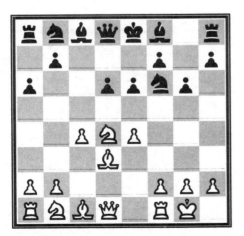

DIAGRAM 124.

7...g6

Diagram 124 shows the *Gipslis Variation*. Black activates his f8-Bishop
by fianchetto, reckoning that the
d6-pawn isn't weak because White
will have to clear the d-file to attack
the pawn. White has the advantage.

Szen Variation

Besides the Paulsen Sicilian, Black
can opt for a different complex
(1.e4 c5 2.Nf3 e6 3.d4 cxd4 4.Nxd4):

4...Nc6

As seen in Diagram 125, Black develops a Knight and doesn't waste a tempo for …a7-a6 yet. As always, the position can allow for a number of transpositions. If White plays 5.Nc3 d6, the game can quickly become a Scheveningen Variation. Black's fourth move distinguishes the *Szen Variation*, which has its own flavor after:

5.Nb5

White makes fast tracks for the d6-square.

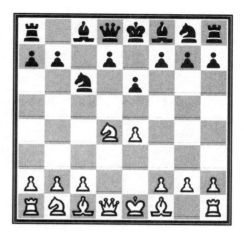

DIAGRAM 125.

5...d6

Black quickly covers his vulnerable square.

6.c4

White once again clamps down on the d5-square.

6...Nf6	**7.N1c3 a6**
8.Na3 Be7	**9.Be2 O-O**
10.O-O	

As shown in Diagram 126, White has control over the d5-square and an advantage in space. But the a3-Knight is misplaced. Practice favors White's position.

Pin Variation

Our final look at the Sicilian complex with …e7-e6 features a provocative line of play by Black (1.e4 c5 2.Nf3 e6 3.d4 cxd4 4.Nxd4):

4...Nf6

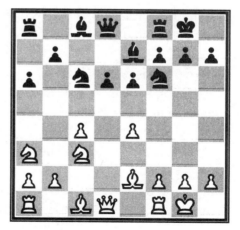

DIAGRAM 126.

147

DIAGRAM 127.

Black immediately attacks the e4-pawn. Because 5.e5? Qa5+ loses a pawn and 5.Bd3 Nc6! 6.Nxc6 dxc6 offers White nothing, White defends the e4-pawn:

5.Nc3 Bb4

Diagram 127 features the *Pin Variation,* which can be quite disconcerting to White when seen for the first time. Fortunately, with correct play, White can gain an advantage:

6.e5! Ne4

It would be a mistake by Black to try to grab material. After 6...Qa5?? 7.exf6! Bxc3+ 8.bxc3 Qxc3+ 9.Qd2! Qxa1 10.c3 Qb1 (Black is worried about 11.Nb3 Qb1 12.Bd3 trapping his Queen) 11.Bd3 Qb6 12.fxg7 Rg8 13.Qh6, White has a winning advantage.

    7.Qg4!

With this key move, White attacks both the e4-Knight and the g7-pawn.

    7...Nxc3   **8.a3 Bf8**
    9.bxc3 Qc7   **10.Qg3**

Despite his damaged pawns, White's lead in development and control of space gives him the advantage.

Bourdonnais Variation

Besides the Sicilian complexes with Black's pawns on either the d6- or e6-squares, one more series of complexes has Black committing his e-pawn to the e5-square. This complex is also very rich and varied (1.e4 c5 2.Nf3):

    2...Nc6   **3.d4 cxd4**
    4.Nxd4 e5

Diagram 128 shows the introductory moves of a whole new complex of Sicilian positions. Black's fourth move is known as the *Bourdonnais Variation* and is quite forcing. White gains nothing from 5.Nxc6? bxc6, when

Black can face the future with confidence. Nor does 5.Nf5? d5! promise any advantage. White's only chance for an advantage is by continuing:

5.Nb5

Black now has three variations that are all quite distinctive:

- 5...a6 (Bourdonnais Variation main line)
- 5...Nf6 (Lasker-Pelikan Variation)
- 5...d6 (Kalashnikov Variation)

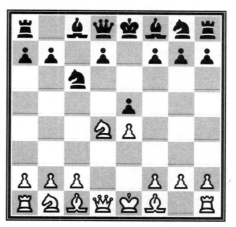

DIAGRAM 128.

In the main line of the Bourdonnais Variation (1.e4 c5 2.Nf3 Nc6 3.d4 cxd4 4.Nxd4 e5 5.Nb5), Black forces White to occupy the d6-square.

5...a6　　　6.Nd6+ Bxd6

7.Qxd6 Qf6

Diagram 129 shows White's befuddlement. He has played natural forcing moves and finds himself without any development. After 8.Qxf6 Nxf6 9.Nc3 d5! 10.exd5 Nb4, Black will favorably recover his pawn. White is better off not trading Queens and instead retreats:

8.Qd1 Qg6　　9.Nc3 Nf6

This leads to an interesting battle with White holding the two Bishops to help him along.

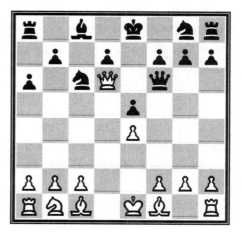

DIAGRAM 129.

DIAGRAM 130.

Lasker-Pelikan Variation

If Black doesn't like giving up the two Bishops as in the Bourdonnais Variation, he can claim them for himself in the *Lasker-Pelikan Variation* (1.e4 c5 2.Nf3 Nc6 3.d4 cxd4 4.Nxd4 e5 5.Nb5):

5...Nf6

This nuance creates a small, but unique, twist.

6.N1c3 d6

Diagram 130 shows how White's Knight has been "forced" to the b5-square. Black intends to play ...a7-a6 and send the b5-Knight into oblivion. White's play is, once more, quite forcing:

7.Bg5 a6   8.Bxf6 gxf6

9.Na3

This has all the makings of a horrible debacle for Black. But wait! We are about to discover a fascinating modern defense:

9...b5

This extraordinary move is called the *Sveshnikov Variation*. White dominates the d5-square and Black practically forces White's Knight to this powerful outpost. But the move has a deeper internal logic. White will have one good d5-Knight, but one bad a3-Knight. Play usually continues:

10.Nd5 f5

Black's plan is to trade off his doubled pawns and, after ...Bf8-g7, to put his two Bishops to work. Modern theory is unsure of its verdict. Practice has shown that Black has fair chances.

Kalashnikov Variation

If the Sveshnikov is too strategically frightening, the *Kalashnikov Variation* is terrifying (1.e4 c5 2.Nf3 Nc6 3.d4 cxd4 4.Nxd4 e5 5.Nb5):

5...d6

With Black's fifth move, shown in Diagram 131, White's Knight is stopped from going to the d6-square. White can try to reinforce his control over the d5-square but Black can fight: 6.Bc4 Be6 7.Bb3 a6 8.N5c3 Nd4 produces an unclear position. Usual is:

6.c4

White brings the c-pawn into the fight for the sweet center. But now the stunning moves that follow create an entirely new struggle:

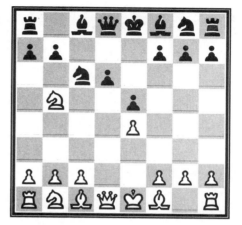

DIAGRAM 131.

6...f5	7.exf5 Bxf5
8.Bd3 Be6	

As you can see from this overview of modern King Pawn defenses, generations of chess players have been busy blazing new and varied trails. Of them all, the Sicilian Defense complexes are the most formidable to master.

Modern Queen Pawn Defenses

A s I demonstrated in Chapter Five, today's grandmasters are willing to experiment with basic principles, oftentimes violating them in order to achieve some other strategic advantages. Recall from Chapter Five how Black would attack White's e4-pawn with ...d7-d5, from the side, so to speak, trying to lure the e-pawn forward. Many of the modern defenses to a Queen Pawn Opening (1.d4) try the same kind of strategy. Other defenses try to ignore the d-pawn and play "around" the center.

Polish Defense

One clear example of playing around the d4-pawn is the *Polish Defense* (1.d4):

1...b5

Black's opening move appears at first to be absurd, but the move has its points: It controls the c4-square and prepares a fianchetto, as shown in Diagram 132.

In 1990 I played a match versus former World Champion Boris Spassky, who three times employed the Polish Defense:

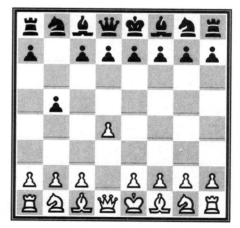

DIAGRAM 132.

153

2.e4 Bb7   3.Bd3 e6
4.Nf3 a6   5.O-O Nf6
6.Re1 c5   7.c3

White has the advantage due to his classical pawn center.

Dutch Defense

The *Dutch Defense* has a goal similar to that of the Polish Defense. Play begins (1.d4):

1...f5

Black isn't trying to meet White in the center. Instead, he's trying to stake out his own territory. It can be argued that the Dutch Defense, shown in Diagram 133, is a bit more sound than the Polish Defense because Black's opening move at least controls the sweet center. Black wants to continue with ...Ng8-f6 and completely control the e4-square.

White can meet the Dutch Defense with a variety of plans. He can fianchetto his King Bishop as in a Catalan. Or he can try any of these options:

- 2.e4 (Staunton Gambit)

- 2.Bg5

- 2.c4 (main line)

Staunton Gambit

If the Dutch Defense sets out to control the e4-square, the *Staunton Gambit* aims to stop Black's plan in its tracks (1d4 f5):

2.e4

White offers his e4-pawn as bait for quick development, as shown in Diagram 134. Black should accept the gambit.

2...fxe4   3.f3

DIAGRAM 133.

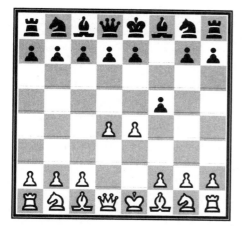

DIAGRAM 134.

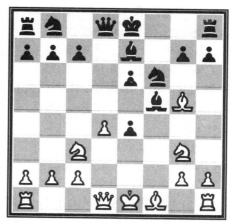

DIAGRAM 135.

White hopes to induce 3...exf3 4.Nxf3 Nf6 5.Bd3 with a promising attack. Black should fall back on his plan of controlling the e4-square:

3...d5	**4.fxe4 dxe4**
5.Nc3 Nf6	**6.Bg5 Bf5**
7.Nge2 e6	**8.Ng3 Be7**

The main line of the Staunton Gambit is shown in Diagram 135. Black continues to control the e4-square and has an acceptable game.

Dutch Defense (2.Bg5)

The Dutch Defense is about controlling the e4-square. White can employ another method to stop the grip (1.d4 f5):

2.Bg5

Displayed in Diagram 136, White's Bishop move is a favorite of mine. Black has a difficult moment. After

DIAGRAM 136.

2…Nf6?! 3.Bxf6 exf6 4.e3, White will play c2-c4 and Nb1-c3 with a sizable advantage. Black's best is:

    2…h6   **3.Bh4 g5**

    4.e3

This opens the evil threat of Qd1-h5 Checkmate!

    4…Nf6   **5.Bg3 Bg7**

    6.Nd2

White has the advantage. Black's Kingside is extended and the move h2-h4 is sure to undermine Black's position.

Dutch Defense, Main Line

If he likes, White can also play into the main line of the Dutch Defense (1.d4 f5):

    2.c4 Nf6   **3.Nc3 e6**

    4.Nf3 Be7   **5.e3 O-O**

    6.Bd3 d5

Black continues his strategy of controlling the e4-square. Black's position is about equal because in this main line, the c1-Bishop has a limited role. Most players like to fianchetto their f1-Bishop as in the Catalan.

DIAGRAM 137.

Modern Queen Pawn Defenses

Of all the modern defenses, Black's most popular opening defensive move is (1.d4):

    1…Nf6

As shown in Diagram 137, Black hasn't committed his central pawns and remains flexible about his intentions. He may soon play …e7-

e6 and ...d7-d5, transposing back into a classical defense. Black waits to see how White intends to continue:

2.c4

This is the starting point for the rest of this chapter. With his second move, White takes up the fight for the center and, given the opportunity, will play Nb1-c3 and e2-e4, occupying the whole center. How will Black stop this plan?

Budapest Gambit

The *Budapest Gambit* was an early favorite of mine (1.d4 Nf6 2.c4):

2...e5

Diagram 138 shows Black's surprising second move. Black attacks the d4-pawn directly. But the e5-pawn is unsupported! White can and should capture the pawn.

3.dxe5 Ng4

Exhibiting a strange leap of faith, Black is forced to move his f6-Knight again, but his aim is to recapture the e5-pawn.

4.Bf4

Naturally, White is quick to protect his gains. An awful mistake would be 4.f4? Bc5, when White has weakened his position. White can also return the gambit pawn by 4.e4 Nxe5 5.f4 Nec6 6.Be3, with a space advantage for White.

4...Nc6   5.Nf3 Bb4+

Now we come to a parting of the ways. White must decide if he'd prefer to play with an extra pawn or with the two Bishops.

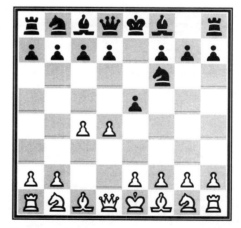

DIAGRAM 138.

Rubinstein Variation

The great Akiba Rubinstein loved the advantage of the two Bishops. He knew how to get 'em and hold 'em (1.d4 Nf6 2.c4 e5 3.dxe5 Ng4 4.Bf4 Nc6 5.Nf3 Bb4+):

6.Nbd2

White blocks the check but allows Black to recapture the gambit pawn:

6...Qe7

Black's move is forced. White threatens 7.h3, with a winning game.

7.a3 Ngxe5

In a stirring moment, Black appears to have lost his senses and left his Bishop en prise. I once watched a tournament game where my friend, Leo Stefurak, cruelly punished his opponent for taking the Bishop: 8.axb4?? Nd3 Smothered Checkmate! What a jolt that was.

8.Nxe5 Nxe5   9.e3

White guards against the Smothered Checkmate.

9...Bxd2+   10.Qxd2

The *Rubinstein Variation* is shown in Diagram 139. White has earned the two Bishops and a small advantage.

DIAGRAM 139.

Budapest Gambit, Main Line

If White wants to hang on to his pawn he can play the Budapest Gambit main line (1.d4 Nf6 2.c4 e5 3.dxe5 Ng4 4.Bf4 Nc6 5.Nf3 Bb4+):

6.Nc3 Bxc3+   7.bxc3 Qe7
8.Qd5

This is the difference: White can protect his e5-pawn.

8...f6

Black can't go fishing for pawns. 8...Qa3? 9.Rc1! Qxa2 10.h3 Nh6

11.e4 gives White a massive advantage.

**9.exf6 Nxf6   10.Qd3 d6
11.g3**

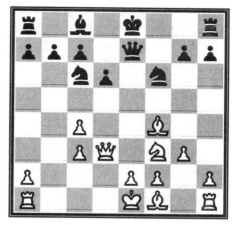

Diagram 140 shows that White has earned the two Bishops *and* an extra pawn. This is why the Budapest Gambit isn't a favorite in master games, but amateurs love its tricky nature.

DIAGRAM 140.

Benko Gambit

One of the most intriguing strategic gambits in opening chess theory is the *Benko Gambit*. Broadly speaking, gambits are sacrifices to gain a short-term edge in development that might be used to win back the sacrificed material. Black usually has a hard time making a gambit work because he is behind a tempo at the start of a game. On the other hand, gambits for White abound, because he has a head start in development. The Benko Gambit doesn't look for a quick reward; it seeks a long-term strategic advantage.

The Benko Gambit begins (1.d4 Nf6 2.c4):

2...c5

Black attacks the d4-pawn from the side. White has several choices. If he plays 3.dxc5 e6, Black will quickly recapture the c5-pawn with a fine game. If White defends the d4-pawn with 3.e3 cxd4 4.exd4 d5, the game has transposed to a Caro-Kann, Botvinnik-Panov Attack. Another choice, 3.Nf3 cxd4 4.Nxd4 a6 5.Nc3 d5, brings Black an easy equality. White's best chance for an advantage is to advance the d-pawn:

3.d5

With this move White is a happy camper. His pawn occupies a fine central square and denies Black's pieces either the c6- or e6-squares.

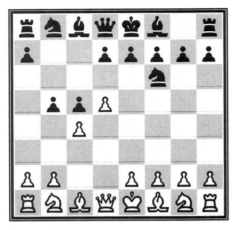

DIAGRAM 141.

3...b5

Diagram 141 shows the starting position of the Benko Gambit. At first the move makes a strange impression. Black is playing on the Queen's wing and not in the center. But the move has great logic. The center is closed for the moment and the c4-pawn, which supports the d5-pawn, is undermined. Whole volumes have been written about whether the Benko Gambit should be accepted or declined. I'll use a page or two to show just few of the main ideas.

Benko Gambit Accepted

The first officially recognized World Champion, Wilhelm Steinitz, once said, "The best way to refute a gambit is to accept it." So that's where we'll start (1.d4 Nf6 2.c4 c5 3.d5 b5):

DIAGRAM 142.

4.cxb5 a6   5.bxa6 Bxa6

The effects of accepting the Benko Gambit can be seen in Diagram 142. Black has developed three units to White's one. Also of great importance is that Black's a8-Rook is ready to pressure the a2-pawn. White's aim will be to catch up in development and defend his d5-pawn.

6.Nc3 g6

This is a crucial link in Black's plans. He wants to fianchetto his King's Bishop so that it too can pressure White's Queenside while offering Black's King a safe haven.

7.g3 d6   8.Bg2 Bg7

9.Nf3 O-O   10.O-O Nbd7

11.Re1

White prepares e2-e4 in an attempt to grab more of the center.

Diagram 143 shows one of the main positions of the Benko Gambit Accepted. Black will play on the Queenside and White in the center. Practice has shown good results for Black and he has full compensation

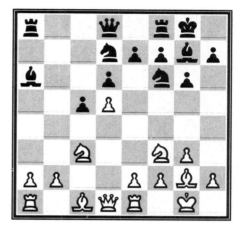

DIAGRAM 143.

for the pawn. This line in no way exhausts the Benko Gambit Accepted possibilities, and I encourage further research.

Benko Gambit Declined

If White isn't happy about accepting the gambit (1.d4 Nf6 2.c4 c5 3.d5 b5), he can always decline it and hope to capture the pawn under better circumstances.

4.Nf3 b4

Black decides not to keep the tension. After 4...bxc4 5.Nc3 d6 6.e4 g6 7.Bxc4, White has a lead in development and a sizable advantage. Black can also choose 4...g6 5.cxb5 a6 6.Nc3 axb5 7.e4!? b4 8.Nb5, with a dangerous attack for White.

5.a3 Na6   6.axb4 Nxb4

7.Nc3 d6   8.e4 g6

White has a strong center in return for allowing the b4-Knight an outpost. Theorists consider the position shown in Diagram 144, on the next page, to be better for White.

DIAGRAM 144.

Benoni Defense

One of the sharpest defenses is the *Benoni Defense*; it's also one of the most difficult to master. A favorite of former World Champion Mikhail Tal, its success even attracted Bobby Fischer to play it against Boris Spassky in their celebrated 1972 World Chess Championship match. The Benoni leads to extremely lively tactical play that keeps both players on their toes. Play begins (1.d4 Nf6 2.c4):

   2...c5   3.d5 e6

Black seeks to remove the cramping d5-pawn.

   4.Nc3 exd5   5.cxd5 d6

Diagram 145 shows the starting position of the Benoni Defense. White has been given a central majority. In return, Black has claimed a Queen-side majority. Both players will use their majorities to control the other player's pieces.

Pawn Storm Variation

The most dangerous weapon in White's arsenal to try to defeat the Benoni is an immediate *Pawn Storm Variation* (1.d4 Nf6 2.c4 c5 3.d5 e6 4.Nc3 exd5 5.cxd5 d6):

   6.e4

White immediately expands in the center. One of Black's aims in the

DIAGRAM 145.

Benoni, as in the Benko Gambit, is to fianchetto his f8-Bishop where it might be more active on the long diagonal. Black starts this strategy now.

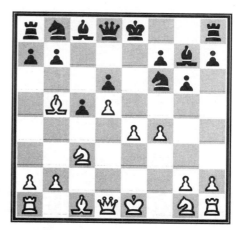

DIAGRAM 146.

6...g6   7.f4

White is planning to blow away the f6-Knight with e4-e5.

7...Bg7   8.Bb5+

This is an important intermezzo move. White would like to play 8.e5 dxe5 9.fxe5 Nfd7 10.e6 fxe6 11.dxe6 Qh4+ 12.g3 Bxc3+ 13.bxc3 Qe4+, but these tactics don't favor him.

The Pawn Storm Variation has reached a pregnant moment, shown in Diagram 146. How will Black handle the check? He has two main choices: 8...Nfd7 and 8...Nbd7.

8...Nfd7

Considered the safe choice, the main line runs:

9.a4

White is worried about ...a7-a6 and ...b7-b5 coming with tempo.

9...Qh4+   10.g3 Qe7
11.Nf3 O-O   12.O-O

This position is considered better for White.

Black's best alternative is (1.d4 Nf6 2.c4 c5 3.d5 e6 4.Nc3 exd5 5.cxd5 d6 6.e4 g6 7.f4 Bg7 8.Bb5+):

8...Nbd7   9.e5 dxe5
10.fxe5 Nh5   11.e6 Qh4+
12.g3 Nxg3   13.hxg3 Qxh1

The tactics of this position, shown in Diagram 147, on the next page, are still being debated, with practice favoring White. This is definitely one variation where preparation is a requirement!

DIAGRAM 147.

Nimzovitch Variation

If the dangers of the Pawn Storm Variation frighten both players, and they should, White can take a more restrained approach by (1.d4 Nf6 2.c4 c5 3.d5 e6 4.Nc3 exd5 5.cxd5 d6):

6.Nf3

White calmly develops his Knight for now.

6...g6

As usual, Black prepares to fianchetto.

7.Nd2

This move distinguishes the *Nimzovitch Variation*, as shown in Diagram 148. White aims to plant his Knight on the c4-square, where it will pressure the d6-pawn.

7...Nbd7

Black intends to meet 8.Nc4 with 8...Nb6, attacking the c4-Knight. Black has also essayed 7...Bg7 8.Nc4 O-O 9.Bf4 Ne8, which is favorable for White.

8.e4 Bg7   **9.Be2 O-O**

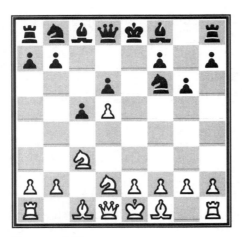

DIAGRAM 148.

10.O-O a6   **11.a4 Re8**

Diagram 149 shows this most topical of Benoni positions. Both players have safe Kings but the strategies for both sides are enormously complex. Practice has shown that the position is double edged but finely balanced.

Modern Variation

Today, the most topical way of meeting the Benoni is (1.d4 Nf6 2.c4 c5 3.d5 e6 4.Nc3 exd5 5.cxd5 d6):

6.e4 g6   7.Nf3 Bg7
8.h3

White rules out ...Bc8-g4 and any trades. White wants to keep pieces on the board due to the cramping effect of his central pawns.

8...O-O   9.Bd3

This modern treatment, shown in Diagram 150, has had a chilling effect on Benoni players. If allowed, White wants to play O-O and Bc1-f4, with an active game. Black tries to counter with an enterprising gambit:

9...b5   10.Bxb5 Nxe4
11.Nxe4 Qa5+   12.Nfd2 Qxb5
13.Nxd6

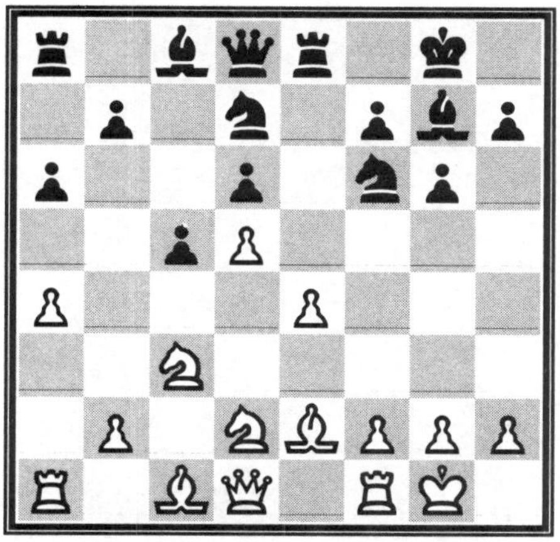

DIAGRAM 149.

Diagram 151 shows the latest word in the modern Benoni theory. The position is a mass of confusion, but for now White has shown a plus in practice.

DIAGRAM 150.

DIAGRAM 151.

DIAGRAM 152.

Czech Benoni Defense

If Black is unhappy about giving White a central majority, he can absolutely lock up the center using a Czech Benoni (1.d4 Nf6 2.c4):

> **2...c5   3.d5 e5**

Instead of challenging White's d5-pawn, Black's e-pawn whizzes right by it. The center now becomes totally blockaded:

> **4.Nc3 d6   5.e4 Be7**

Diagram 152 shows he starting position of the *Czech Benoni Defense.*

White has a fine wedge in the center which cramps Black pieces, but how will he further exploit it? With the center so locked, play on the flanks becomes all important. The main line of the Czech Benoni is an intriguing line:

> **6.h3**

Concerned that Black will be able to make trades after 6.Nf3 Bg4, White makes a precautionary move.

> **6...O-O   7.Nf3 Ne8**

Black is preparing to play ...f7-f5 to attack White's center.

> **8.g4**

White attempts to put a stop to Black's plan.

> **8...Nd7   9.Bd3 g6**

Black refuses to flinch away from his plan.

> **10.Bh6 Ng7   11.Rg1 Nf6**
> **12.Qe2 Kh8   13.O-O-O Ng8**
> **14.Bd2 f5   15.gxf5 gxf5**

Diagram 153 shows that, at long last, Black has gotten in his King-side break. But who benefits from the open lines? Theory favors White but the practical results show that Black has chances too.

Nimzo-Indian Defense

While the Sicilian Defense is the granddaddy of modern King Pawn Defenses, the *Nimzovitch-Indian* (or *Nimzo-Indian*) is the granddaddy of Queen Pawn Defenses. The amount

DIAGRAM 153.

of chess literature written about this defense is astounding. While writing this book, I entered this section with trepidation. I cannot possibly cover the myriad ideas of the Nimzo-Indian in such a work. Rather, I can form an impression for you and encourage you to make further research yourself.

As shown in Diagram 154, the Nimzo-Indian is reached by (1.d4 Nf6 2.c4):

2...e6

Black doesn't yet take a firm stand in the center as with the Budapest Gambit or the Benoni Defense. Rather, he simply opens up the diagonal for the f8-Bishop. White continues his standard development.

3.Nc3 Bb4

This is Nimzovitch's idea. The c3-Knight is pinned, making the move e2-e4 difficult to carry out. On the other hand, Black is showing a will-

DIAGRAM 154.

ingness to part with the two Bishops early in the game. Black hopes that if he is to lose his Bishop he will have the satisfaction of doubling White's pawns. White has tried a variety of moves, including:

- 4.Bg5 (Leningrad Variation)
- 4.a3 (Samisch Variation)
- 4.Qb3 (Spielmann Variation)
- 4.Qc2 (Classical Variation)
- 4.e3 (Rubinstein Variation)

Leningrad Variation

If Black is going to pin White's Knight, it's only fair that White might return the favor (1.d4 Nf6 2.c4 e6 3.Nc3 Bb4):

4.Bg5

White pins Black's Knight and hopes to play e2-e4 in the near future. This line is called the *Leningrad Variation*, and it was a great favorite of former World Champion Boris Spassky.

4...c5	**5.d5 h6**
6.Bh4 Bxc3+	**7.bxc3 d6**

DIAGRAM 155.

Now that Black has traded away his dark squared Bishop, he quickly puts his center pawns on the dark squares where they will not obstruct his c8-Bishop.

8.e3

White has to go slowly in the center. The immediate 8.e4? g5 will cost him the e4-pawn.

8...e5	**9.f3**

Diagram 155 shows a main position from the Leningrad Variation. Black has done a good job of clogging up the center. White's Bishops aren't working at the moment. Practice has favored Black!

Samisch Variation

If Black is willing to part with the two Bishops, White reasons that he should force him to do so (1.d4 Nf6 2.c4 e6 3.Nc3 Bb4):

4.a3

White puts the question to the Black Bishop and obliges the capture:

4...Bxc3+ 5.bxc3

DIAGRAM 156.

Diagram 156 shows the starting position of the *Samisch Variation*. White has a nice grouping of pawns, even if they are doubled. Black's strategy is to freeze the c4-pawn so that he might capture it in the near future:

5...c5

White now faces a crucial decision as to how to play in the center. Should he play 6.e3 and slowly prepare the advance of his e-pawn, or should he play 6.f3 and play for e2-e4 in one go?

Samisch Variation (6.e3)

If White goes slowly with his e-pawn, Black has time to organize a counterattack against the c4-pawn (1.d4 Nf6 2.c4 e6 3.Nc3 Bb4 4.a3 Bxc3+ 5.bxc3 c5):

6.e3

White intends to develop his Kingside pieces before pushing through in the center.

6...Nc6	**7.Bd3 O-O**
8.Ne2 b6	**9.e4 Ne8!**

Diagram 157, on the next page, displays the fine idea of Jose Raul Capablanca, the third World Champion. Black prevents a possible Bc1-g5, which

DIAGRAM 157.

puts his Knight in an unpleasant pin. Furthermore, Black gets his pieces out of the way of White's imposing pawn center. Left to his own devices, Black intends to play ...Bc8-a6, ...Nc6-a5 and possibly ...Ne8-d6, clipping the c4-pawn. Practice has favored Black once more.

Samisch Variation (6.f3)

The modern way to play the Samisch Variation is (1.d4 Nf6 2.c4 e6 3.Nc3 Bb4 4.a3 Bxc3+ 5.bxc3 c5):

6.f3

White wastes no time, but immediately goes for his e2-e4 set-up. Black feels obliged to halt White in the center.

6...d5   7.cxd5 Nxd5

White would have an advantage after 7...exd5 8.e3 O-O 9.Bd3 b6 10.Ne2 Ba6 due to his extra pawns in the center. Mikhail Botvinnik was an excellent champion of White's possibilities in this position.

8.dxc5

Owing to his two Bishops, White tries to open up the position as much as possible. As soon as he plays e2-e4, he can count on a plus.

8...f5

As shown in Diagram 158, Black tries to put a stop to e2-e4 and expects to round up the c5-pawn in the near future by playing ...Nb8-

DIAGRAM 158.

a6. The position is absolutely devilish and requires careful study. The position is dynamically balanced.

Spielmann Variation

In the Nimzo-Indian, the doubled c-pawns can be downright annoying. It begins to make sense that White should avoid the doubled pawns, and what could be more natural than (1.d4 Nf6 2.c4 e6 3.Nc3 Bb4):

4.Qb3

DIAGRAM 159.

Diagram 159 shows the starting position of the *Spielmann Variation*. White not only stops his pawns from becoming doubled, he even attacks the b4-Bishop with tempo! What could be sweeter? The only problem with this move is that the Queen becomes a tactical target.

4...c5

Black protects his Bishop and attacks the d4-pawn. If White plays 5.a3? Bxc3+ 6.Qxc3 cxd4 7.Qxd4 d5 8.Nf3 Nc6, Black will have the advantage.

5.dxc5 Nc6

Black now has the annoying threat of ...Nc6-d4, which pushes White's Queen away from the protection of the c3-Knight.

6.Nf3 Ne4!   **7.Bd2 Nxc5**

Black can also play 7...Nxd2. In both cases Black's chances are good.

Classical Variation

You should now realize some of the problems that White has handling the Nimzo-Indian. A much favored continuation even to this day is the *Classical Variation* (1.d4 Nf6 2.c4 e6 3.Nc3 Bb4):

4.Qc2

With this quiet move, White reinforces his c3-Knight and prepares both a2-a3 and e2-e4 with fine gains. Black has three main choices: 4...c5, 4...d5 and 4...O-O.

Classical Variation (4...c5)

A completely reasonable reaction for Black is to attack White's center at once (1.d4 Nf6 2.c4 e6 3.Nc3 Bb4 4.Qc2):

4...c5

Now that the d5-square isn't supported by White's Queen, the d-pawn can't be pushed.

5.dxc5 O-O

Black can also consider the sharp line 5...Na6 6.a3 Bxc3+ 7.Qxc3 Nxc5 8.b4 Nce4 9.Qd4 d5 10.c5 b6, which is still in great debate.

6.a3 Bxc5	**7.Nf3 Nc6**
8.Bg5 Nd4	**9.Nxd4 Bxd4**
10.e3 Qa5	**11.exd4 Qxg5**
12.Qd2	

This famous ending from the Classical Nimzo is shown in Diagram 160. Practice has shown an advantage for White.

DIAGRAM 160.

Classical Variation (4...d5)

One of the sharpest lines of the Classical Variation is shown after (1.d4 Nf6 2.c4 e6 3.Nc3 Bb4 4.Qc2):

4...d5

Black takes a stand in the center.

5.a3 Bxc3+	**6.Qxc3 Ne4**
7.Qc2 Nc6	**8.e3 e5**

Diagram 161 shows the starting position of what is sometimes called the *Grand Variation*. Watch what happens now:

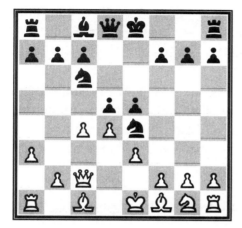

DIAGRAM 161.

DIAGRAM 162.

9.cxd5 Qxd5	10.Bc4 Qa5+
11.b4 Nxb4	12.Qxe4 Nc2++
13.Ke2 Qe1+	14.Kf3 Nxa1

Diagram 162 shows the starting position for this Grand Variation. Modern practice favors White and it is an excellent position to play with your friends. What do *you* think is going on? This is one of those positions where general principles are replaced by concrete analysis.

Classical Variation (4...O-O)

A far more topical treatment of the Classical Defense is to allow White to win the two Bishops (1.d4 Nf6 2.c4 e6 3.Nc3 Bb4 4.Qc2):

4...O-O

As shown in Diagram 163, Black safely tucks his King away before starting aggressions in the center.

5.a3

DIAGRAM 163.

White is sorely tempted to play 5.e4, gaining ground in the center, but 5...d5 6.cxd5 exd5 7.e5 Ne4 8.Bd3 c5! gives Black excellent counter chances. With the text White claims the two Bishops.

5...Bxc3+   6.Qxc3 b6

Black prepares to fianchetto his c8-Bishop and control the e4-square. In this way the Nimzo-Indian gets its name. At the turn of the century the fianchetto was simply called "irregular" and later was referred to as an "Indian" development by the hypermodernists who began experimenting with all kinds of openings and defenses.

7.Bg5 Bb7

Many grandmaster games today begin this way. The position shown in Diagram 164 is considered dynamically equal.

Rubinstein Variation

Somehow White's play against the Nimzo-Indian hasn't been altogether convincing. The Samisch Variation only seems to encourage Black's intentions, and the Classical Variation has White spending a lot of tempi with his Queen to avoid doubled pawns. Another approach seems to be needed. Once again Akiba Rubinstein offered a solution (1.d4 Nf6 2.c4 e6 3.Nc3 Bb4):

4.e3

Diagram 165 shows the *Rubinstein Variation*. As mentioned in the section on the Budapest Gambit, Akiba loved the Bishops. White plans to play Ne2 and put the question to the b4-Bishop. Black has tried 4...b6 (Bronstein Variation), 4...c5 (Huebner Variation), 4...d5, and 4...O-O. Naturally, each defensive try has its own peculiarities.

DIAGRAM 164.

Rubinstein Variation, Bronstein Variation

David Bronstein, virtual co-champion of the world in 1951, is a player with enormous creative gifts. He has enriched practically every opening he ever played. This is the *Bronstein Variation* (1.d4 Nf6 2.c4 e6 3.Nc3 Bb4 4.e3):

4...b6

It is quite witty. Black realizes that White intends to win the two Bishops and so prepares to trade one away.

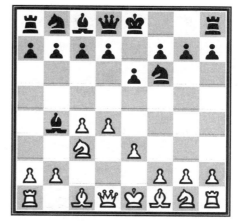

DIAGRAM 165.

5.Nge2 Ba6   6.a3 Bxc3+
7.Nxc3 d5

Bronstein's idea can be seen in Diagram 166.

8.b3 Nc6

Black intends to play ...Nc6-a5, pressuring the c4-pawn. White has a small advantage.

Rubinstein Variation, Huebner Variation

In my view, the best way for Black to meet the Rubinstein Variation is with the line introduced by German grandmaster Robert Huebner (1.d4 Nf6 2.c4 e6 3.Nc3 Bb4 4.e3):

4...c5

Diagram 167, on the next page, shows Huebner's idea. He wants to start a quick attack on White's center. White has two choices: He can

DIAGRAM 166.

175

DIAGRAM 167.

play 5.Ne2, continuing with the idea of winning the two Bishops, or he can play for development with 5.Bd3.

Rubinstein Variation, Huebner Variation (5.Ne2)

In the next two moves, White completes his idea of winning the two Bishops.

5.Ne2 d5		**6.a3 Bxc3+**	
7.Nxc3 cxd4		**8.exd4 dxc4**	

Black makes all these trades in the center to force White to have an isolated Queen pawn.

9.Bxc4 O-O   10.O-O Nc6

11.Be3 b6

White's position in Diagram 168 is a favorite of Victor Kortchnoi. White has an advantage of the two Bishops, but after fianchettoing Black will have good chances to equalize.

DIAGRAM 168.

Rubinstein Variation, Huebner Variation (5.Bd3)

If White isn't satisfied by his edge in Diagram 168, he can try a different piece arrangement (1.d4 Nf6 2.c4 e6 3.Nc3 Bb4 4.e3 c5):

5.Bd3

White decides to develop his Bishop first, anticipating that he will have a better chance for e3-e4 in the future.

5...Nc6

In Diagram 169, White faces a crucial decision. Where should his g1-
Knight go, to the e2- or f3-square?

DIAGRAM 169.

Rubinstein Variation, Huebner Variation (6.Nge2)

In this variation, White plays in the
classical manner preferred by Akiba
Rubinstein (1.d4 Nf6 2.c4 e6 3.Nc3
Bb4 4.e3 c5 5.Bd3 Nc6):

6.Nge2

Left to his own devices, White will
castle and play d4-d5 with an over-
whelming position. Black is quick to respond in the center.

6...cxd4	**7.exd4 d5**
8.a3 dxc4	**9.Bxc4 Be7**

Another typical isolated Queen pawn middle game has emerged in Diagram 170. Practice has favored White because it is easy for him to play d4-
d5 with advantage due to his superior development.

Rubinstein Variation, Huebner Variation (6.Nf3)

In Diagram 170, the e2-Knight isn't
well placed, and many grandmasters prefer the traditional f3-square
(1.d4 Nf6 2.c4 e6 3.Nc3 Bb4 4.e3 c5
5.Bd3 Nc6):

6.Nf3

White invites the same kind of isolated Queen pawn as in the previous
line and expects his Knight to be better placed. Black changes his plan:

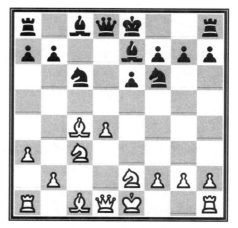

DIAGRAM 170.

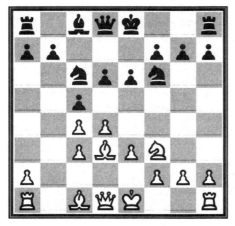

DIAGRAM 171.

6...Bxc3+   7.bxc3 d6!

Black's shift of plan is shown in Diagram 171. He intends to block the center with ...e6-e5, when White's Bishops will have difficulty activating themselves.

8.O-O e5   9.Nd2!

White makes a surprising, yet powerful, retreat. White wants to launch his f2-pawn into the central fray.

9...O-O

It would be a mistake for Black to capture the d4-pawn with 9...cxd4 10.cxd4 exd4 11.exd4 Nxd4 12.Bb2 Ne6 13.Ne4, leaving White's Bishops to radiate their power.

10.d5 Ne7   11.Qc2

White is prepared to play f2-f4, with good chances for the initiative. Black will try to keep the position blocked so that White's Bishops can't cooperate. Practice has shown the position to be balanced, although Black must play with great care.

Rubinstein Variation (4...d5)

So far against the Rubinstein Variation, we have looked at Bronstein's and Huebner's ideas. After White has committed himself to e2-e3, it is far more natural for Black to respond in the center in classical style (1.d4 Nf6 2.c4 e6 3.Nc3 Bb4 4.e3):

4...d5

As shown in Diagram 172, Black wants to keep the e4-square as well covered as possible. If he can stop White from playing e3-e4, the c1-Bishop will be deprived of a future!

5.a3 Bxc3+

Black can also retreat with 5...Be7 6.Nf3 O-O 7.b4, giving White an edge in the center and the Queenside, but without giving up the two Bishops.

6.bxc3 c5

This attack in the center is necessary. One day White will play c4xd5 and then use his newly minted c3-pawn as a central battering ram.

7.Bd3 O-O   8.Ne2 b6

Black seeks an active diagonal for his Bishop. This move is the signal

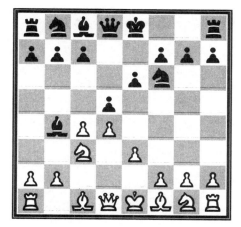

DIAGRAM 172.

for White that the time has come to trade his c4-pawn.

9.cxd5 exd5   10.Ng3

Compare Diagram 173 with the note on the Samisch Variation. It is a direct transposition. As previously mentioned, Mikhail Botvinnik liked to play White's position as he would play f2-f3 and Ne2-g3, building up the break e3-e4. White has an advantage.

Rubinstein Variation (4.O-O)

The last look at the Rubinstein Variation analyzes the most popular defense (1.d4 Nf6 2.c4 e6 3.Nc3 Bb4 4.e3):

4...O-O

As shown in Diagram 174, on the next page, Black whips his King to safety and retains all the flexible defensive options previously mentioned. He hasn't committed his central pawns and may play with

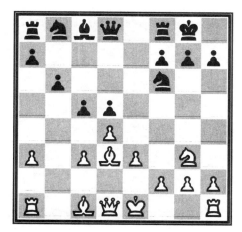

DIAGRAM 173.

179

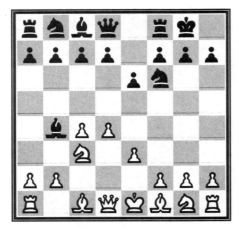

DIAGRAM 174.

...d7-d5 or ...d7-d6, putting his central pawns on light or dark squares. From Diagram 174, White must decide between 5.Ne2 (*Reshevsky Variation*) and 5.Bd3.

Rubinstein Variation, Reshevsky Variation

Like Akiba Rubinstein, Samuel Reshevsky loved the two Bishops. His favorite line was (1.d4 Nf6 2.c4 e6 3.Nc3 Bb4 4.e3 O-O):

5. Nge2

White immediately goes for a2-a3 so that he can recapture the Bishop with his Knight. Black is now forced to respond in the center:

5...d5   6.a3 Be7

Black has been forced into this retreat. Black can also play 6...Bd6 7.c5 Be7 8.b4, allowing White to gain space on the Queenside.

7.Nf4

DIAGRAM 175.

Reshevsky made a career out of the position shown in Diagram 175. White has the advantage.

Rubinstein Variation (5.Bd3)

The most analyzed continuation of the Rubinstein Variation is (1.d4 Nf6 2.c4 e6 3.Nc3 Bb4 4.e3 O-O):

5.Bd3

White hasn't committed his Knight and wants to see how Black will respond in the center.

5...c5   6.Nf3 d5

7.O-O dxc4   8.Bxc4 b6

Diagram 176 represents a starting position of the Rubinstein Variation. The options are quite complex, and I encourage further study! Black's last move plans ...Bc8-a6, trading White's best piece. Most games continue:

9.Qe2 Bb7   10.Rd1

A fine battle lies ahead.

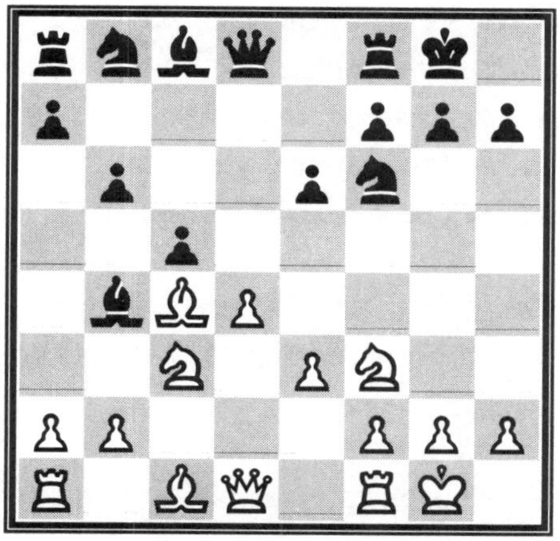

Bogo-Indian Defense

DIAGRAM 176.

If the White player finds himself overwhelmed by the complexities of the Nimzo-Indian, he can duck the line on move three (1.d4 Nf6 2.c4):

2...e6   3.Nf3

As Diagram 177 shows, White doesn't allow the Nimzo-Indian. Instead, he invites his opponent to play 3...d5, transposing back to a classical Queen Pawn Defense, or 3...c5 4.d5, transposing back to a Benoni Defense. Many grandmasters appreciate these transpositions. They feint with a Nimzo-Indian only to transpose to a Benoni. In this way certain lines, such as the Pawn Storm in the Benoni, are averted. If Black doesn't want to transpose back into these defenses, he can give the position its own flavor by playing:

3...Bb4+

This variation is attributed to Efim Bogoljubow. When faced with a last name like that, it is easy to see why

DIAGRAM 177.

181

players called this defense the *Bogo Variation*. Because Black often fianchettos his Queen's Bishop, the defense became known as the *Bogo-Indian Defense*. If White doesn't want to play 4.Nc3, transposing back into the Nimzo-Indian, he should block Black's check in one of two ways: 4.Nbd2 or 4.Bd2 (the main line).

Bogo-Indian Defense (4.Nbd2)

My favored continuation is to block Black's check with (1.d4 Nf6 2.c4 e6 3.Nf3 Bb4+):

4.Nbd2

My reasoning is simple: I want to play a2-a3 and win the two Bishops as in a classical Nimzo-Indian without spending tempi with my Queen. If Black doesn't give up the two Bishops, my d2-Knight will support e2-e4.

4...b6

This is a key move to understanding the Bogo-Indian. Black tries to control the e4-square with pieces and not by playing ...d7-d5, which requires him to commit himself in the center.

5.a3 Bxd2+

Practically speaking, this capture is forced. After 5...Be7 6.e4 Bb7 7.Bd3, White has control over the e4-square and a clear advantage.

6.Qxd2

Diagram 178 shows this paradoxical capture. After 6.Nxd2 Bb7, White will have to spend time blocking the long diagonal. After 6.Bxd2 Bb7, it isn't clear what White should do with his dark-squared Bishop. In a few moves, White's plan will be clear:

6...Bb7   7.e3 O-O

DIAGRAM 178.

Black could play 7...Bxf3 8.gxf3, but White will soon play Bf1-g2 and f3-f4, with a powerful middle game.

8.Be2 d6   9.O-O Nbd7
10.b4!

Diagram 179 shows how the middle game plans for both sides begin to take shape. White intends to fianchetto his dark-squared Bishop for good central control. Black intends to occupy the e4-square with his Knight and follow up with ...f7-f5 to play on the light squares. Practice has favored White.

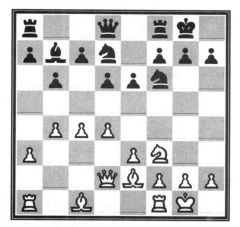

DIAGRAM 179.

Bogo-Indian Defense, Main Line

Black's Bishop check has provoked a response and it's certainly natural to rebuff the impudent attacker with an attack of your own (1.d4 Nf6 2.c4 e6 3.Nf3 Bb4+):

4.Bd2

This is the main line of the Bogo-Indian, and it's a completely logical counter. If Black is forced to trade Bishops, White's development would get a boost.

4...Qe7

Not wishing to help White develop, Black defends his Bishop. Black has also tried 4...a5 and 4...c5, but the text is the most logical.

Diagram 180 shows White's strategic problem in a different light.

DIAGRAM 180.

What will White do with his f1-Bishop? The c4-pawn means that the f1-a6 diagonal isn't the brightest, so White decides on a fianchetto.

5.g3

It also might seem like a reasonable plan to play for e2-e4. After trading a few pieces with 5.Nc3 Bxc3 6.Bxc3 Ne4 7.Qc2 Nxc3 8.Qxc3 d6 9.e4 Nd7, Black will play for ...e6-e5 with rough equality.

5...Nc6   6.Bg2 Bxd2+

Black chooses the right moment to trade Bishops. White can't play 7.Qxd2?! Ne4 8.Qc2 Qb4+, which gives Black the initiative.

7.Nbxd2 d6

Diagram 181 is typical of the Bogo-Indian. Black has the flexibility to change plans. He now plans ...e6-e5 in order to activate his c8-Bishop.

8.O-O e5   9.d5

White gains a nice wedge in the center.

9...Nb8   10.e4

Diagram 182 shows the starting position for most grandmaster games with the Bogo-Indian. White's central control gives him the advantage, but Black's position is quite solid. Black will play ...Nb8-a6, thereby controlling the c5-square.

DIAGRAM 181.

DIAGRAM 182.

Queen's Indian Defense

By now you've observed that learning all the plans of a Nimzo-Indian is a daunting challenge to the White player. Gaining a spatial advantage against the Bogo-Indian isn't as difficult, so Black sets up a new challenge, the *Queen's Indian Defense*. In this defensive scheme, Black quickly fianchettos his Queen's Bishop.

The Queen's Indian Defense is initiated after the moves (1.d4 Nf6 2.c4):

2...e6   3.Nf3 b6

As shown in Diagram 183, Black prepares to fianchetto his Queen's Bishop in order to control the e4-square. This strategy is typical of modern defenses. While White's pawns *occupy* the center, Black's pieces *control* the central squares.

From Diagram 183, White has taken a number of approaches:

- He would like to play e2-e4, so 4.Nc3 (the Botvinnik Variation) is a logical continuation. Unfortunately, this move allows Black's f8-Bishop to pin the c3-Knight, just as in a Nimzo-Indian.

- To avoid the pin, White has taken the time to prepare the development of his Knight by first playing 4.a3 (the Petrosian Variation).

- White's main move in the Queen's Indian is to play 4.g3, countering Black's fianchetto with one of his own.

DIAGRAM 183.

Botvinnik Variation

Mikhail Botvinnik had a deserved reputation as an "iron logician," a player whose purposeful moves followed a completely logical

185

DIAGRAM 184.

sequence. The following variation of the Queen's Indian Defense bears his name (1.d4 Nf6 2.c4 e6 3.Nf3 b6):

4.Nc3

White revs up to play e2-e4 for central domination.

4...Bb4

Just as in the Nimzo-Indian, Black is quick to make this pin.

5.Bg5

White counters with a pin of his own.

5...Bb7

Black continues to observe the e4-square.

6.e3

White intends Bf1-d3, in order to complete his development and tussle for control over the e4-square.

6...h6   7.Bh4 g5

Black breaks the pin but weakens his Kingside in the process.

8.Bg3 Ne4   9.Qc2 Bxc3+

10.bxc3 Nxg3   11.hxg3 d6

Diagram 184 features the starting position of the Queen's Indian Botvinnik Variation. Many grandmaster games have been played from this position as both sides have strengths and weaknesses. Practice has favored White but not by much.

Petrosian Variation

The ninth World Champion, Tigran Petrosian (1929–84, World Champion 1963–69), had an extraordinary gift for frustrating his opponents' plans. Grandmaster Robert Byrne once commented to me, "Petrosian would play a defensive combination long before his opponent realized he had a chance to attack!" He mastered the art of *prophylaxis*, anticipating the dangerous plans of his opponent before they could arise. His specialty was to carefully prepare his advances, nurturing and building his position before initiating a clash. He conjured up the following variation (1.d4 Nf6 2.c4 e6 3.Nf3 b6):

4.a3

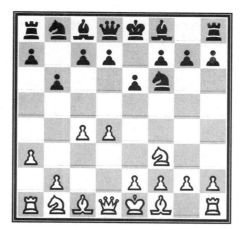

DIAGRAM 185.

Diagram 185 shows the *Petrosian Variation*. White spends a whole tempo in the opening to prevent the pin in the Botvinnik Variation.

4...Bb7   5.Nc3 d5

At last Black has been provoked into committing himself in the center. White was threatening to play d4-d5 and e4-e5, completely shutting out the b7-Bishop.

6.cxd5 Nxd5

After 6...exd5, the position becomes that of a Queen's Gambit Declined. The text gives this variation its unique flavor.

7.Qc2

White is playing for e2-e4. Early in his career, Garry Kasparov's favorite weapon as White was this position. Practice has favored White.

Queen's Indian Defense, Main Line

The most popular way for White to meet the Queen's Indian is to fianchetto his own Bishop (1.d4 Nf6 2.c4 e6 3.Nf3 b6):

4.g3

White reasons that if Black just tries to play with his pieces, his position will invariably become cramped. At some point, Black will have to commit

DIAGRAM 186.

his central pawns; in the meantime, White has a safe haven for his King on the Kingside.

4...Bb7

An entirely different idea of the Queen's Indian is for Black to change his approach and target the c4-pawn. Black reasons that if White is going to fianchetto his f1-Bishop, the c4-pawn might be vulnerable: 4...Ba6 5.b3 c6 6.Bg2 d5 reaches a position that is also favored in grandmaster chess.

5.Bg2 Be7   6.O-O O-O

Diagram 186 shows the starting position for the main line Queen's Indian Defense. Most games continue by 7.Nc3 Ne4 8.Qc2 Nxc3 9.Qxc3 f5, both players contending for control of the e4-square. Vladimir Kramnik, currently the world's third highest-rated grandmaster, prefers 7.Re1, waiting to see how Black will react. The Queen's Indian Defense is considered one of the most solid defensive systems available against the Queen Pawn Opening.

Grunfeld Defense

The last modern defense against the Queen Pawn Opening I consider in this survey is the *Grunfeld Defense*. More than any other modern defensive scheme, the Grunfeld typifies piece play for Black and occupation of the center by White. The opening moves are (1.d4 Nf6 2.c4):

2...g6

This time Black decides to fianchetto his own King's Bishop.

3.Nc3

White is ready to play e2-e4 with central domination.

3...d5

Black makes a surprising move by striking in the center. It is Black's third move that initiates the *Grunfeld Defense*, which is shown in Diagram 187.

White has three main responses to the Grunfeld Defense:

- 4.cxd5 (Exchange Variation)
- 4.Nf3 (Three Knights Variation)
- 4.Bf4

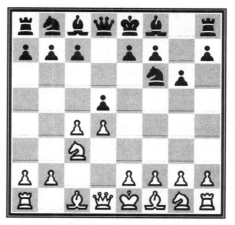

DIAGRAM 187.

Exchange Variation

The most logical continuation for White, and hence the one that has the largest body of theory, is the *Grunfeld Exchange Variation* (1.d4 Nf6 2.c4 g6 3.Nc3 d5):

4.cxd5

Naturally, White is pleased at the prospect of exchanging a flank pawn, the c4-pawn, for Black's central pawn.

4...Nxd5   5.e4 Nxc3
6.bxc3

Diagram 188 shows the starting position for the Grunfeld Exchange Variation. Naturally, White is very pleased with himself. He has established a classical center in exactly half a dozen moves. Classical players are cheering! But Black isn't about to give up the game now. He reasons that after fianchettoing his Bishop, he

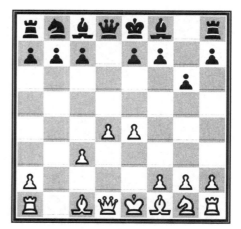

DIAGRAM 188.

will be able to put strong pressure on White's d4-pawn and the long diagonal. Play now continues:

6...Bg7

Black plans the counter ...c7-c5 and ...Nb8-c6 to attack the d4-pawn. White must make a crucial decision as to how he should defend his center. Would he like his Knight defending his d4-pawn on the e2- or f3-square? While the f3-square is preferable, the Knight would then be vulnerable to a pin from the c8-Bishop.

Exchange Variation, Main Line

For several decades the main line of the Exchange Variation was the standard (1.d4 Nf6 2.c4 g6 3.Nc3 d5 4.cxd5 Nxd5 5.e4 Nxc3 6.bxc3 Bg7):

7.Bc4

White develops a Bishop while making room for the g1-Knight to have a comfortable development.

7...c5

Once more, Black strikes into the center. The pressure of the g7-Bishop on the long diagonal is making itself felt.

8.Ne2

DIAGRAM 189.

This was White's development scheme. On the e2-square, the Knight is not vulnerable to the c8-Bishop.

8...O-O   9.O-O Nc6
10.Be3

Both players have followed their plans in exemplary fashion. White occupies the center and therefore should be pleased with his game. But the fight is just beginning! From Diagram 189, play proceeds:

10...Bg4

This move appears to be a wasted effort because White can easily neutralize the pin. Black's move has a deeper point.

11.f3 Na5

This is Black's point: the move f2-f3 weakens White's position.

12.Bd3

Practically a whole FIDE World Championship Match between Anatoly Karpov and Garry Kasparov was contested after 12.Bxf7+ Rxf7 13.fxg4 Rxf1+ 14.Kxf1. Today this line is con-

DIAGRAM 190.

sidered completely equal and thus preference is made for the text.

12...cxd4   13.cxd4 Be6

The position shown in Diagram 190 is considered a key starting point for the Grunfeld Exchange Variation. Having provoked the move f2-f3, Black clearly wants to play ...Na5-c4, attacking the vulnerable e3-Bishop. Dozens of games have been played that feature the exchange sacrifice, 14.d5 Bxa1 15.Qxa1 f6 16.Bh6 Re8, with Black usually doing well! Modern players now play:

14.Rc1 Bxa2   15.Qa4 Bb3
16.Qb4 b6

White has excellent compensation for the pawn and practice has shown the position to be about equal.

Exchange Variation, Modern Line

Today's grandmasters have devised a new approach to the Exchange Grunfeld that involves placing the King's Knight more aggressively (1.d4 Nf6 2.c4 g6 3.Nc3 d5 4.cxd5 Nxd5 5.e4 Nxc3 6.bxc3 Bg7):

7.Nf3

DIAGRAM 191.

Diagram 191 shows the more combative approach. Modern players have devised a way of meeting the ...Bc8-g4 pin.

> **7...c5   8.Rb1**

And this is it. The b7-pawn needs protection and the c8-Bishop is to be kept at home. If Black tries to block the Rook's attack, 8...b6 9.Bb5+ disrupts Black's plans of attacking the d4-pawn.

> **8...O-O   9.Be2 cxd4**
> **10.cxd4 Qa5+   11.Bd2**

Once more, White offers his a2-pawn as a gambit. The ending after 11.Qd2 Qxd2+ 12.Bxd2 b6, preparing ...Bc8-b7, is considered harmless for Black.

> **11...Qxa2**

The position shown in Diagram 192 is quite the rage in grandmaster circles. Results have favored White in a series of tactical melees. Do your research and come prepared to your tournament games!

Three Knights Variation

If the amount of analysis of the Exchange Variation seems overwhelming, the *Three Knights Variation* might be easier (1.d4 Nf6 2.c4 g6 3.Nc3 d5):

> **4.Nf3**

White calmly develops a Knight and chooses not to define the center just yet.

DIAGRAM 192.

4...Bg7

Now White must reveal his plans. He can play 5.cxd5, transposing into the Exchange Grunfeld, and play the modern line. Or he can choose one of the following variations, which have their own flavor:

- 5.Qb3 (Russian Variation)
- 5.Bg5 (Seirawan Variation)

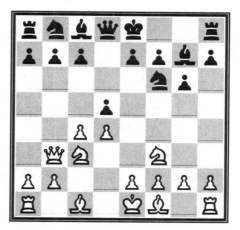

DIAGRAM 193.

Three Knights Variation, Russian Variation

The Russian school of chess has done an amazing "joint collaboration" on the following bottomless variation (1.d4 Nf6 2.c4 g6 3.Nc3 d5 4.Nf3 Bg7):

5.Qb3

As shown in Diagram 193, White develops his Queen early in order to put pressure on Black's d5-pawn. White realizes that after the passive move 5...c6 6.cxd5 cxd5, the game will become an Exchange Slav Defense, with Black's fianchetto misplaced. The standard moves are:

5...dxc4   6.Qxc4 O-O
7.e4

Diagram 194 shows the current position. White has achieved a classical pawn center but the premature development of his Queen means that Black can create all kinds of counter defenses. Just to list the *main variations:*

DIAGRAM 194.

193

- 7...a6 (Hungarian Variation)
- 7...Na6 (Prins Variation)
- 7...b6 (Levenfish Variation)
- 7...c6 (Lundin Variation)
- 7...Nc6 (Simagin Variation)
- 7...Bg4 (Smyslov Variation)

All of these variations have their unique qualities and books have been written about their strengths and weaknesses. While I believe that the Smyslov Variation makes the most sense, others may properly disagree. Let me just say that all of these lines are fascinating and the ideas challenging.

Three Knights Variation, Seirawan Variation

With so many complex lines to choose from, I decided to create a simple "anti-Grunfeld" weapon that I've used with great success. I even defeated Garry Kasparov in the Chess Olympics with the following (1.d4 Nf6 2.c4 g6 3.Nc3 d5 4.Nf3 Bg7):

5.Bg5

From the position shown in Diagram 195, White plans to eliminate the f6-Knight and grab the d5-pawn.

DIAGRAM 195.

5...Ne4

This is the best move. After 5...dxc4? 6.e4!, White will favorably recover the c4-pawn. Another alternative, 5...c6 6.cxd5 cxd5 7.e3, once again is an Exchange Slav Defense where the g7-Bishop bites on granite, and with the d4-pawn, White has the advantage.

6.cxd5 Nxg5!

Black properly snares the two Bishops. After 6...Nxc3 7.bxc3 Qxd5

8.e3, White has more influence in the center, and once more the g7-Bishop has a limited future.

7.Nxg5 e6   8.Nf3

This latter move was really my concept. Previously White players had tried 8.Qd2 exd5 9.Qe3+ Kf8 10.Qf4 Bf6!, but hadn't received an advantage.

8...exd5   9.b4

Diagram 196 shows the *Seirawan Variation*. The game is similar to a Queen's Gambit Declined, where

DIAGRAM 196.

White has played Bc1-g5xf6, giving up the two Bishops for a Queenside minority attack.

9...O-O   10.e3

Black's g7-Bishop is on a closed diagonal. Practice favors White.

Grunfeld Defense (4.Bf4)

This last look at the Grunfeld features another logical move that ignores the action in the center (1.d4 Nf6 2.c4 g6 3.Nc3 d5):

4.Bf4

White develops his Bishop and targets the c7-pawn.

4...Bg7   5.e3

This is crucial to White's opening strategy. The Bishop is developed outside of the pawn chain and reinforces the d4-pawn. Diagram 197 shows the position, with Black hav-

DIAGRAM 197.

ing to choose between 5...c6, 5...c5, and 5...O-O.

5...c6

This passive move doesn't suit the nature of the Grunfeld Defense. White can trade by 6.cxd5 cxd5, with a favorable Exchange Slav, or he can continue:

6.Nf3 O-O   7.Bd3

White has the advantage.

Far more common is (1.d4 Nf6 2.c4 g6 3.Nc3 d5 4.Bf4 Bg7 5.e3):

5...c5

Black tries to blast open the long diagonal for the g7-Bishop.

6.dxc5 Qa5

Black prepares a possible ...Nf6-e4 to attack the c3-Knight.

7.Rc1 dxc4   8.Bxc4 O-O

9.Nf3 Qxc5

White has a lead in development that gives him a slight advantage.

Grunfeld Gambit

An intriguing gambit appears after (1.d4 Nf6 2.c4 g6 3.Nc3 d5 4.Bf4 Bg7 5.e3):

DIAGRAM 198.

5...O-O

White can now play 6.Rc1, with a likely transposition to the line given above. The text move has independence if White decides to gobble a pawn:

6.cxd5 Nxd5   7.Nxd5 Qxd5

8.Bxc7

White has won the c7-pawn, as shown in Diagram 198. Black's compensation after 8...Na6 9.Bg3 Bf5 is quite visible. A difficult ending, however, arises in Diagram 198 after 8...Na6 9.Bxa6 Qxg2 10.Qf3 Qxf3 11.Nxf3 bxa6, which favors White.

This completes our survey of the major modern defenses to the Queen Pawn Opening. I hope I've provided you with food for thought and that you now have a better understanding of the reasons *behind* most chess openings.

CHAPTER SEVEN

An Opening Solution

U nderstanding the information presented in the previous chapters took me several years. Learning all the classical openings and defenses and their names was a real bear. It did, however, help me to appreciate that I'd never return to my Cannon or Queen Raid Openings! My favorite opening move became 1.e4, and it would have stayed that way forever except for one small problem: I lost. In fact, I lost quite often and the opening was the real culprit. It seemed to me that it was necessary to become a specialist in every opening and defense! As soon as I'd find a line to deal with the Dragon, I lost because I wasn't aware of the latest wrinkle in the Scheveningen Keres Attack. Things didn't get better with the Petroff Defense. Not knowing the nuances of so many openings meant that I couldn't get an edge, no matter which line I chose. My complaints only got affirmative nods, "Yep, you're right Yaz. Let me know when you find something good."

In a strange way that I couldn't articulate, it seemed to me that after a few years of playing chess, I was playing less "original" chess in my games. I'd play the first dozen or so opening moves as prescribed by the great chess teachers and end up with either a completely won position or a bad one that I couldn't hold. Much like the fellow who checkmated me in four moves and exclaimed that I had been his fourth victim, my opponents at this time would tell me that I had fallen into the same trap as their previous opponent. It didn't make me feel any better!

I realized that I wanted to play a game of chess that had less of a "theoretical" understanding. My friends called this approach "getting out of book"—the *book* being the rather large body of opening theory. But how on earth could I escape? The whole purpose of opening theory was to prescribe the best set of opening moves and counters so that a player would have a decent middle game position. Didn't getting out of book mean being at a disadvantage? After all, I'd no longer be following the recommended moves of top grandmasters. The answer is a succinct no. There is no single best opening or best defense. As this book has already shown, there are hundreds to choose from. What is important is finding an opening and defense that is comfortable for you—one where you can understand the formation and the plans that will give you the type of position that you want.

Building a House

What I discovered for myself is that, despite my choice of opening or defense, I often left my own King vulnerable. I was so locked in on targeting my opponent's King that I constantly left my own inadequately protected. In attacking the Dragon Sicilian, I noted that the g7-Bishop—besides putting pressure on the long diagonal—is a great defender. The concept of *building a house* took root, and that's exactly what I did.

Building a house is making a fianchetto and sliding your King underneath the Bishop. Once my King was nicely protected, only then did I start to worry about the center. Experienced players who are reading this book have probably noticed that the previous chapters on classical openings missed the Barcza Opening and the English Opening, and the chapters on modern defenses overlooked the King's Indian Defense and the Pirc Defense. These omissions were deliberate, because these openings are the ones I recommend.

When I decided to avoid opening theory, it took me a long time to give up 1.e4 because this move seemed like a trusted old friend. Instead my new move order would be:

1.Nf3

Instead of trying to occupy the center with either 1.e4 or 1.d4, my new opening move was the start of my house building. The move controls the d4 and e5-squares and leaves it up to Black to choose his defense.

    1...Nf6   **2.g3**

This was the second step in building my house. The Bishop is to be fianchettoed on the long diagonal.

    2...g6

Black does the same thing.

    3.Bg2 Bg7   **4.O-O O-O**

In Diagram 199, we see that both sides have built homes for their Kings. Both have a solid pawn shield and are covered by a Knight, a Bishop, and a Rook. It was from this formation that I realized it was possible to simply play chess without any disadvantages from not knowing the opening. The center is still left to be defined, but my King was nice and safe and I could face the future with confidence.

Barcza Opening

Gedeon Barcza (1911–86) was a Hungarian grandmaster who enjoyed play-

ing the "quiet" opening moves shown in Diagram 199. Against nearly every Black defense, White's first four moves were always the same. Only after the King was tucked away did White turn his attention to the center. My joy for chess was rekindled after I started to play the *Barcza Opening*. No longer did I have to know the latest wrinkle of an Open Ruy Lopez. I could now try to outplay my opponent with both of us playing our own moves.

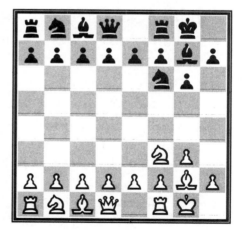

DIAGRAM 199.

Just about every World Champion at one time in their careers has played the Barcza Opening. Garry Kasparov used it against Deep Blue in their celebrated 1997 match. The world's third highest-rated grandmaster, Vladimir Kramnik, has used it throughout his entire career. Although the opening often transposes into other openings and defenses, this choice is entirely White's.

White's four opening moves, 1.Nf3, 2.g3, 3.Bg2, and 4.O-O, create the Barcza Opening. After these initial moves, if White follows up with c2-c4, the opening often transposes into an English Opening. If he plays d2-d4, a likely transposition into a Catalan will occur. And if White plays for d2-d3 and e2-e4, the opening becomes a *King's Indian Attack (KIA)*. The KIA became my favorite because the ideas are quite easy to grasp.

Now that we know what we are going to do as White, we need a few strategies to play against Black's reactions. Black often stakes out the center, and these are the variations for which we need ideas to combat:

- The Barcza Opening is often met by the London Defense: 1...d5, 2...Nf6, 3...Bf5 or 3...Bg4.

- Black can play to occupy the center with a King's Indian Reversed Defense: 1...d5, 2...c5, 3...Nc6, 4...e5.

- Black can also play to occupy the center with 1...d5, 2...c5, 3...Nc6, 4...e6, which White should take into a Closed French Defense.

- Black can copy White's opening (see Diagram 199), and then I recommend a King's Indian Attack.

- Finally, Black can fianchetto his Queen's Bishop as in the Queen's Indian Defense. This is called the Hedgehog Defense. Once more, the King's Indian Attack is the winning formula.

London Defense (...Bc8-f5)

As its name suggests, the *London Defense* is a venerable one noted for its solidity. Black opens with his Queen Pawn and develops in classical fashion while White plays the Barcza setup:

1.Nf3 d5   2.g3 Nf6

As so often happens in openings, Black's first two moves are often interchanged.

3.Bg2 Bf5   4.O-O

These moves lead to the position shown in Diagram 200.

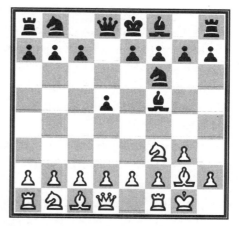

White has built his house and now needs to find a plan. Black has developed three of his units, which all control the sweet center. In fact,

DIAGRAM 200.

all three of Black's pieces control the e4-square. Good for him! So what should White's plan be? The King's Indian Attack is based upon White trying to push his e2-pawn up the board. White aims to do this by playing d2-d3 and Nb1-d2, preparing the charge of his e-pawn.

4...e6

Black fortifies the d5-pawn and makes room for the f8-Bishop. Note that Black has developed the f5-Bishop outside of his pawn chain.

5.d3

This is the signal move for the KIA. White could have played 5.c4, 5.d4, or 5.b3, each of which would channel the game in a different direction. The text move retains White's flexibility to choose another plan, but it does show that White is preparing e2-e4.

5...h6

This move has become the standard for Black. It is interesting to note that despite the lead that Black held in controlling the e4-square, White will be able to push his e-pawn forward. That being the case, Black prepares the h7-square as a retreat square.

6.Nbd2

This is not the ideal square for the Knight because it blocks the c1-Bishop. But White is counting upon the move e2-e4 to provide him with breathing room in the future. The development of the c1-Bishop is delayed. If White wants he can also fianchetto his Queen's Bishop.

6...Be7

Black is happy to develop and to prepare to castle.

7.b3

Once more White prepares another fianchetto.

7...O-O   8.Bb2 Nbd7

9.Re1

The position is shown in Diagram 201.

White is now prepared to push his e-pawn up the board with tempo. He can then play for a Kingside attack by playing e4-e5 to push away the f6-Knight, or by playing in the center. White's good Bishops and flexible position gives him the advantage in a position where neither player needs to worry about the latest theoretical wrinkle.

London Defense (...Bc8-g4)

In this line of the London Defense, Black plays an important nuance by

developing his Bishop to the g4-square. Often this results in a trade for the f3-Knight. In such cases, its important that Black keep the long diagonal blocked; otherwise the g2-Bishop becomes extremely powerful.

1.Nf3 Nf6   2.g3 d5

3.Bg2 Bg4

One of the goals behind Black's strategy is to capture White's f3-Knight and follow up with ...e7-e5 in

DIAGRAM 201.

an attempt to establish a classical pawn center.

4.O-O Bxf3

Black immediately captures the Knight.

5.exf3

I prefer this recapture, as shown in Diagram 202. After 5.Bxf3 e5, Black gets to implement his plan. With 5.exf3, Black's center quickly collapses after 5...e5? 6.Re1 Nc6 7.d4! Black isn't able to play ...e7-e5 and must content himself with simple developing moves:

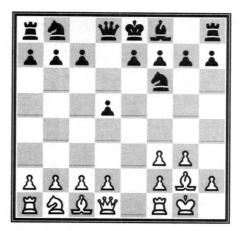

DIAGRAM 202.

    5...e6   **6.f4**

With this excellent move, White opens the long diagonal and tightens down on the e5-square, which will become a natural outpost.

    6...Be7   **7.d3 O-O**

    8.Nd2 c5

Black takes a risk that he might not be able to keep the long diagonal closed. While 8...c6 is more solid, it is passive.

    9.Nf3 Nc6   **10.Re1**

White will soon post a Knight on the e5-square and have a small advantage.

King's Indian Reversed Defense (...d5xe4)

If the Barcza Opening has a drawback, it is that Black is given the opportunity to occupy the center at once. A classical player quickly picks up on this opportunity. White will be placed in the position of a counterattacker, which he will have to play forcefully:

    1.Nf3 d5   **2.g3 c5**

    3.Bg2 Nc6   **4.O-O e5**

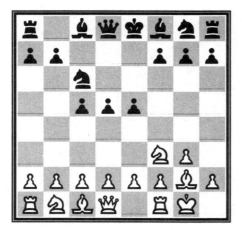

DIAGRAM 203.

Black now occupies the entire center, as shown in Diagram 203. Once again, White will play to get in e2-e4 and his own play in the center.

5.d3

White protects himself against any plans of ...e5-e4 and prepares his counter.

5...Nf6   6.e4

With this key move, White attacks the d5-pawn and forces Black to make a decision. Does he capture the e4-pawn by 6...dxe4? Push his pawn with 6...d4? Or continue his development by 6...Be7? The choice isn't an easy one.

6...dxe4

At first glance, this move appears to win a pawn, but appearances are deceiving. White's e4-pawn is inviolate:

7.dxe4 Qxd1   8.Rxd1 Bg4

Black correctly refrains from "winning" the e4-pawn with 8...Nxe4? 9.Nxe5 Nxe5 10.Bxe4. White has won back his pawn and has the much superior position as he has a lead in development. He will try to bring his Knight to the d5-square and play Bc1-f4, developing with tempo.

9.c3

An excellent move as White prevents any play based upon ...Nc6-d4, trying to take advantage of the pin created by Black's last move. This position is considered quite favorable to White due to the *pawn structure*. I describe the concept of pawn structure extensively in *Play Winning Chess* (Microsoft Press, 1995) and *Winning Chess Strategies* (Microsoft Press, 1994). Black's d5-square is vulnerable to invasion, while White's d4-square is not.

The position, shown in Diagram 204, should be studied closely because this formation is quite common in a King's Indian Reversed. My suggestion is to play the position out against friends as well as against a computer. Once again the e4-pawn can't be captured:

9...Nxe4?   10.Re1

DIAGRAM 204.

Now Black is in trouble. The Knight retreating by 10...Nf6 11.Nxe5 is excellent for White. If Black plays 10...Bxf3 11.Bxf3 Nf6 12.Bxc6+, White again reclaims his pawn with advantage.

10...f5   11.Nh4

This fine stroke decides the position in White's favor. He is threatening f2-f3, where he wins a piece, as well as Nh4xf5—with or without h2-h3—when White will reclaim his pawn with advantage.

King's Indian Reversed Defense (...d5-d4)

As you've just witnessed, capturing the e-pawn works badly for Black. He therefore decides to close the center (1.Nf3 d5 2.g3 c5 3.Bg2 Nc6 4.O-O e5 5.d3 Nf6 6.e4):

6...d4

Diagram 205 shows the position. With the center pawns locked, play on the flanks becomes the leading factor. White will play for the breaks f2-f4 and c2-c3 to pressure the

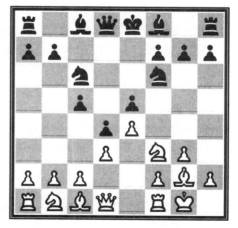

DIAGRAM 205.

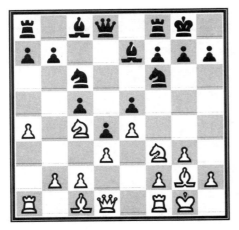

DIAGRAM 206.

center. One of the benefits to White after Black's last move is that he now has control over the c4-square, which provides him with an ideal outpost for the b1-Knight.

7.a4

This appears to be a strange move until you understand the idea behind the move. White is anticipating playing Nb1-a3-c4. Once he has spent so much time traveling there, he doesn't want his arrival to be greeted by ...b7-b5 giving the Knight the boot. White thus secures the c4-outpost for his Knight.

7...Be7	**8.Na3 O-O**
9.Nc4	

The game has evolved to the position shown in Diagram 206.

9...Nd7	**10.Ne1**

White is ready to play f2-f4 and a possible Kingside pawn storm. Once again, White is considered to possess a positional advantage.

King's Indian Reversed Defense (...Bf8-e7)

Clearly, Black isn't entirely satisfied with the above two lines. On move six he tries a different plan (1.Nf3 d5 2.g3 c5 3.Bg2 Nc6 4.O-O e5 5.d3 Nf6 6.e4):

6...Be7

Instead of capturing the e4-pawn or bypassing with the d-pawn, Black just develops. Now White takes a different approach from the position shown in Diagram 207.

7.exd5

White opens the long diagonal for his g2-Bishop and exposes the e5-pawn to a frontal attack.

7...Nxd5

In such positions, recapturing with the Queen is extremely dangerous due to the potential of a discovered attack by the g2-Bishop.

8.Re1

White immediately puts pressure on the e-pawn.

8...f6

Black does not make this move happily, but 8...Bf6 9.Nxe5 Nxe5 10.f4 is good for White, while 8...Qd6 invites 9.Nbd2, with the threat of Nd2-c4 winning a pawn.

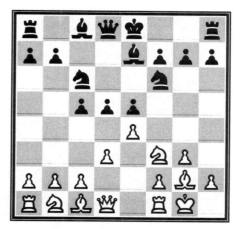

DIAGRAM 207.

9.c3

White is preparing to open the position to his advantage with d3-d4.

9...O-O 10.d4

This position, shown in Diagram 208, will soon clarify into White's favor due to his good g2-Bishop and the weaknesses caused by the move ...f7-f6.

Closed French Defense

If Black tries to occupy the center, but doesn't want to weaken his d5-square, he can try a different formation (1.Nf3 d5 2.g3 c5 3.Bg2 Nc6 4.O-O):

4...e6

DIAGRAM 208.

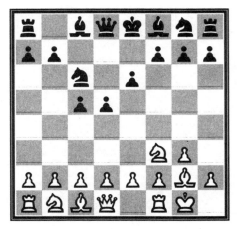

DIAGRAM 209.

Black is happy with his central gains and plays to strengthen his center. The position is shown in Diagram 209.

By now White's play should be quite familiar. He will again use his e-pawn as a battering ram.

5.d3 Nf6   6.Nbd2 Be7
7.e4 O-O

As White, this was one of Bobby Fischer's favorite positions, which he used to score a number of fine wins. While the center is not locked, it soon will be. The players pursue different plans: White will go Kingside, Black Queenside.

8.Re1 b5

Black gains space on the Queenside while planning to launch a pawn storm.

9.e5 Nd7   10.h4

This is a key move in White's plan of attacking Black's King. The g5-square is to be used as a likely stepping stone and the h2-square is cleared for reasons that will soon become apparent:

10...b4   11.Nf1 a5
12.N1h2 a4   13.Bf4

Practice has shown that White has the better chances.

Hedgehog Defense

Black's final defensive reaction that I'll examine is the *Hedgehog Defense*. Black meets White's Kingside fianchetto with a Kingside fianchetto in order to neutralize the g2-Bishop:

1.Nf3 c5   2.g3 b6

This move initiates the Hedgehog.

3.Bg2

This is a position where White should carefully consider his move order. He could play 3.e4 Bb7 4.d3, setting up a King's Indian Attack at once and thereby limiting Black's choices.

3...Bb7   4.O-O g6

In Diagram 210 we can see Black's strategy. He plans to fianchetto both his Bishops and leave it up to White to define the center.

5.d3 Bg7   6.e4 d6

DIAGRAM 210.

Black plays cautiously, obviously having been previously victimized by a King's Indian Attack!

7.Nbd2 Nd7   8.Re1 Ngf6

9.c3 O-O

The game has evolved to Diagram 211. White can play for d3-d4 and push in the center. The Hedgehog is one of the best ways for Black to meet the Barcza Opening.

Certainly, by adopting the Barcza Opening as White, you will cut out a number of losses that you would experience by playing complicated classical openings. Your need to know the theoretical lines is reduced and you can be quite confident in the safety of your King.

DIAGRAM 211.

CHAPTER EIGHT

A Solution to the Queen Pawn Opening

I was so attracted to the Barcza Opening as White that I tried out the same formation as Black against White's Queen Pawn Opening. Known as the *King's Indian Defense (KID)*, this is the favorite defense of both Garry Kasparov and Bobby Fischer. It comes highly recommended! Let's see it in action:

1.d4 Nf6	**2.c4 g6**
3.Nc3 Bg7	**4.e4 d6**

Of course, White is under no obligation to occupy the center. He can play much more quietly with his first four moves, but it is these opening moves that put the most pressure upon Black's formation.

Diagram 212 serves as the starting position. White has a large number of choices. White's main tries are:

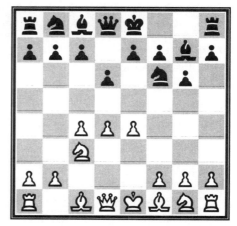

- 5.f4 (Four Pawns Attack)

- 5.f3 (Samisch Variation)

- 5.Be2 (Averbach Variation)

- 5.Nf3 (main line)

Four Pawns Attack

One of Black's greatest fears in playing the King's Indian Defense is the

DIAGRAM 212.

DIAGRAM 213.

Four Pawns Attack (1.d4 Nf6 2.c4 g6 3.Nc3 Bg7 4.e4 d6):

5.f4

As shown in Diagram 213, White's pawn center is quite imposing! What's worse from Black's perspective, the routine of ...d7-d6 and ...e7-e5 has been severely disrupted, and it is now impossible for Black to count on this maneuver. A change of plans is needed—and fast. However, don't despair! Although White has occupied the center, his pawns can easily become overextended.

5...c5

Black immediately attacks White's center and forces him to make a decision.

6.d5

White bypasses the c5-pawn. After 6.dxc5 Qa5!, Black threatens ...Nf6xe4, with a winning attack. White has to protect the e4-pawn: 7.Bd3 Qxc5 produces a crucial recapture. White is prevented from playing e4-e5 in the future, and play continues: 8.Nf3 O-O 9.Qe2 Bg4 10.Be3 Qa5 11.O-O Nc6. Practice has shown the position to be dynamically equal.

6...O-O   7.Nf3

White must be careful not to overextend his center. A mistake would be 7.e5? Ne8 8.Nf3 Bg4, when White's center collapses under Black's pressure.

7...b5!

Black makes a necessary pawn sacrifice that is similar to the Benko Gambit. Diagram 214 shows the position.

Black desperately, and correctly, tries to break up White's center. White must accept the sacrifice because ...b5-b4 threatens to win the e4-pawn.

8.cxb5

After 8.e5 dxe5 9.fxe5 Ng4! 10.Bf4 b4 11.Ne4 Nd7, Black is well placed to meet White in the center.

8...a6　　　9.a4

White decides to cling to his extra pawn.

9...Nbd7　　　10.Be2 axb5

11.Bxb5 Ba6

Practice has shown that Black has compensation for his pawn. He will try to utilize the half-open b-file to create counterplay.

DIAGRAM 214.

Samisch Variation

Another aggressive system against the KID is the *Samisch Variation* (1.d4 Nf6 2.c4 g6 3.Nc3 Bg7 4.e4 d6):

5.f3

In this variation, White's intentions are cleverly disguised. At the position shown in Diagram 215, White wants to play Bc1-e3, Qd1-d2, and castle long. He will attack on the Kingside in a style similar to the Yugoslav Attack of the Sicilian Dragon.

Because I like to play the Samisch Variation as White, I know that Black has to play carefully to gain a safe position. However, the Samisch Variation has an important drawback. In the words of

DIAGRAM 215.

215

grandmaster Eduard Gufeld, "Please, ask the g1-Knight how he likes the move f2-f3. He has been robbed of his best square!"

5...e5

This is probably the only time that Black should make this move *before* castling—an important nuance. Black is not worried about the ending 6.dxe5 dxe5 7.Qxd8+ Kxd8 8.Bg5 c6 9.O-O-O+ Kc7, correctly believing that this middle game is not worse for him.

6.d5

This is considered White's best chance of gaining an advantage. Recall from considering the Barcza Opening that a line like 6.Nge2 exd4 7.Nxd4 O-O 8.Be2 c6 has Black preparing the break ...d6-d5, with a fine game.

6...Na6

Once again, Black plays for the positional plan of controlling the c5-square. When the colors were reversed, White prefaced this move with a2-a4.

7.Be3

White sets up the attacking line previously outlined.

7...Nh5

This move has a dual purpose: It clears the way for Black to play ...f7-f5 and possibly ...Qd8-h4+ in order to disrupt White's plan.

DIAGRAM 216.

8.Qd2

Diagram 216 shows one of the most interesting variations of the KID. Black can now play 8...f5, a key source of counterplay in the KID that gives him a fair game. Or he can try the *Bronstein Variation:*

8...Qh4+   9.Bf2 Qf4

Black invites White to trade Queens if he'd like.

10.Be3 Qh4+

This invites a repetition, which is declined as follows:

11.g3 Nxg3   12.Qf2

Certainly White must avoid 12.Bf2? Nxf1, which would result in the loss of a pawn for White. Now, however, Black is forced to sacrifice his Queen:

12...Nxf1   13.Qxh4 Nxe3

Black has the threats of ...Ne3-g2+ and ...Ne3-c2+, so White now moves his King:

14.Ke2 Nxc4

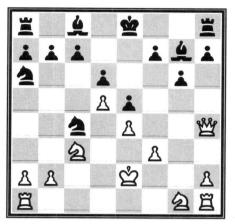

DIAGRAM 217.

As shown in Diagram 217, Black has a material deficit of two Bishops and two pawns for his Queen. Speaking bluntly, the position is absolutely gross and defies analysis. I've played Black's position against Kasparov and made an easy draw. Players who don't like to sacrifice their Queen should play 8...f5 instead. But please, do yourself the favor of playing out this position against a friend. It will be very rewarding. Play often continues:

15.b3 Nb6   16.Rc1 Bd7

17.Nh3 O-O   18.Nf2 f6

19.a4 Rae8

A fascinating game lies ahead. Clearly, the Samisch Variation is quite a challenging one for Black and he must be on his toes.

Averbach Variation

The purpose of f2-f3 in the Samisch Variation is to set up with Bc1-e3 and prevent ...Nf6-g4, which would harass White's Bishop. Isn't there another way White can do this without playing f2-f3? With this move, White covers the g4-square and initiates the *Averbach Variation* (1.d4 Nf6 2.c4 g6 3.Nc3 Bg7 4.e4 d6):

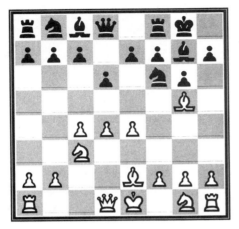

DIAGRAM 218.

5.Be2

The move is highly transpositional and we haven't reached the Averbach Variation quite yet.

5...O-O   6.Bg5

This is the move that signals the Averbach Variation, as shown in Diagram 218.

White's sixth move is far more annoying than 6.Be3, because on the g5-square, the Bishop is far more active. When Black plays his freeing move ...e7-e5, he will place himself in a nasty pin.

6...c6

Black prepares to counter in the center. The immediate 6...e5? 7.dxe5 dxe5 8.Qxd8 Rxd8 9.Nd5 would be a failure as Black loses material.

7.Qd2 e5

Now this break works because the d5-square is covered.

8.d5 cxd5   9.cxd5

While it might be tempting to capture on d5 with the Knight, it is wrong; after playing 9.Nxd5 Nc6 10.O-O-O Be6, Black's Knight goes to the d4-square and Black earns a good game.

9...Nbd7 10.f3

In view of Black's impending pressure on the e4-pawn with ...Nd7-c5, White strengthens his center.

10...a5

As before, Black secures the c5-square.

11.Nh3 Nc5   12.Nf2 a4

13.O-O Bd7

Theorists consider the position shown in Diagram 219 to be dynamically balanced.

King's Indian Defense, Main Line

By far, White's most popular way of meeting the KID is the main line, where White just develops his King-side, happy with his central gains (1.d4 Nf6 2.c4 g6 3.Nc3 Bg7 4.e4 d6):

    5.Nf3 O-O   **6.Be2**

DIAGRAM 219.

White's last two moves are inter-changeable and some grandmasters enjoy the time their opponents spend reflecting about how they intend to meet the Averbach Variation!

    6...e5   **7.O-O**

Diagram 220 features the starting position of the main line King's Indian Defense. My colleague, grandmaster John Nunn, has written two 300-page books called *The Main Line King's Indian* (Henry Holt and Company, 1996) and *The New Classical King's Indian* (International Chess Enterprises, 1997), in which he goes into great detail about the strategic considerations facing both players. Needless to say, it is an impossible act to follow! My recommendation for Black is to play as follows:

    7...exd4   **8.Nxd4 Re8**
    9.f3 c6

DIAGRAM 220.

219

DIAGRAM 221.

Black is ready to break out with ...d6-d5 or, at certain times, ...Qd8-b6, which can be an annoying move.

10.Kh1

This is the key move in this variation, as shown in Diagram 221.

White has tried other lines, including 10.Be3 and 10.Nc2, and is unable to gain any superiority. (One nice trick for Black is 10.Be3 d5 11.cxd5 Nxd5! 12.Nxd5 cxd5, leaving Black with no problems.) Instead, White gets off the a7-g1 diagonal where his King might be vulnerable.

10...Nbd7

This is considered the most solid continuation. Black would dearly love to play the immediate ...d6-d5, but it fails: 10...d5 11.cxd5 cxd5 12.Bg5 dxe4 13.Ndb5! White's lead in development gives him the advantage. With the text, Black is prepared to put his Knight on either the e5- or c5-square and, in the cases of ...d6-d5, the Knight can play to the b6-square.

White now has a large choice of moves, including 11.Nb3, 11.Nc2, 11.Rb1, and 11.Bf4. Theory considers this to be White's best move:

11.Bg5

The f6-Knight is pinned and Black's ability to play ...d6-d5 is slowed.

11...h6

Black also has his choices, and 11...Qb6 and 11...Qa5 have been popular alternatives. I prefer the text for reasons that shall soon be clear:

12.Bh4 Ne5   13.Qc2

One trick that White must avoid is 13.Qd2? Nxe4! because the h4-Bishop is unprotected.

13...g5   14.Bf2 c5
15.Nb3 Be6

These moves lead to the position shown in Diagram 222. Theory considers White's position to be slightly better, but I'm suspicious of this evaluation. Benoni players will be happy to have a powerful e5-Knight, and the b3-Knight is definitely out of play for some time. Black is certainly capable of raising a heck of a fuss. Take a close look at this position and see how much fun playing the KID can be!

DIAGRAM 222.

CHAPTER NINE

A Solution to the King Pawn Opening

A fter discovering the solidity of building a house in chess, I became attracted to the very same formations against White's King Pawn Opening. This time, however, the ideas were far more tricky for me than in a Barcza Opening and a King's Indian Defense (KID). In time, I learned to play the *Pirc Defense*, which became a career defense that I still use to this day. The opening move order is quite important for Black as a single mistake can give him a bad game.

The opening moves are:

1.e4 d6

Black is heading for the Barcza formation. The alternative 1...Nf6 is the Alekhine Defense, which would provoke e4-e5—a threat Black will try to avoid.

2.d4

White establishes a classical pawn center. White could certainly entertain other, quieter formations, but this is considered White's best.

2...Nf6

Black develops while attacking the e4-pawn.

3.Nc3

White could also play 3.f3 g6 4.c4 Bg7 5.Nc3, transposing directly back to the Samisch Variation of the KID. In fact, this was the move order that Kasparov used against me in one of our tournament games.

3...g6

Black initiates the Pirc Defense. Left to his own devices, Black will complete his house and then counter in the center. From the position shown

DIAGRAM 223.

in Diagram 223, White has a wide range of possibilities:

- 4.f4, called the Austrian Attack or the Three Pawns Attack, is the most dangerous for Black. White tries to prevent ...e7-e5 and often plays for e4-e5, booting away the f6-Knight and trying to disturb Black's house.

- 4.f3 or 4.Be3 prepares the development of his c1-Bishop so he can castle Queenside and conduct an attack similar to the Yugoslav Attack in the Sicilian Dragon.

- 4.Bg5 is currently a popular system for White. Aiming for Qd1-d2 and Bg5-h6 to trade dark-squared Bishops, this line is called the Modern System.

- 4.Be2 launches a credible attacking idea similar to the Averbach Variation in the KID. White plays for h2-h4-h5, trying to blow down Black's house.

- 4.Nf3, the main line (also called the Geller Variation) focuses on White's desire to complete his Kingside development and hold a plus in the center.

In comparing Diagram 223 with Diagram 212, the difference is the placement of White's c-pawn. It can be argued that the pawn on the c4-square is far more active and controls the sweet center. On the c2-square, White's Queenside isn't as weakened, so that if White decides to castle there, his King's protection will be significantly improved. The difference comes down to a question of style. One thing is certain: With the pawn on c2, White can use the extra tempo to considerably sharpen the game.

Austrian Attack

The *Austrian Attack* causes Black to be on guard early. Play begins (1.e4 d6 2.d4 Nf6 3.Nc3 g6):

4.f4

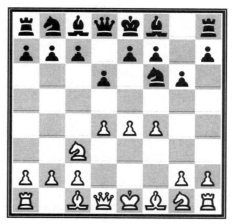

DIAGRAM 224.

Diagram 224 shows the initial position of the Austrian Attack, and it's easy to see why it's also called the *Three Pawns Attack*. White's play is straightforward as can be; he is winding up for e4-e5 and crashing through in the center.

4...Bg7   5.Nf3 O-O

These moves lead to the most provocative lines of the Austrian. White is being encouraged to push in the center, where Black hopes that White will become overextended. White now has three main lines:

- 6.e5, accepting the central challenge

- 6.Bd3, preparing to quickly castle Kingside

- 6.Be3, intending e4-e5 and central domination

Austrian Attack (6.e5)

The central push seems logical, but Black should be happy because he can chip away at White's center (1.e4 d6 2.d4 Nf6 3.Nc3 g6 4.f4 Bg7 5.Nf3 O-O):

6.e5 Ne8

Black is forced to retreat, but in so doing opens the way for his g7-Bishop. Black's central focus will be the e5-pawn, and he'll use ...c7-c5 to undermine White's central support.

7.Be3

White develops and tries to restrain the ...c7-c5 break. White has tried 7.Bc4, 7.Bd3, and 7.h4, but in each case 7...c5 gives Black good counterplay.

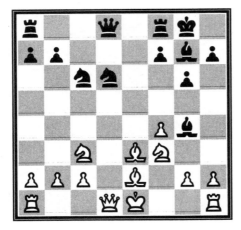

DIAGRAM 225.

12.Bc5 Bxc3+   13.bxc3 Ne4
14.Bxf8 Qb6

After Black's fourteenth move, he has gained a dangerous attack. A likely continuation is 15.Rf1 Nxc3 16.Qd2 Nxe2 17.Qxe2 Rxf8, when Black has sacrificed an exchange for good play against White's King.

DIAGRAM 226.

7...c5   8.dxc5
White accepts Black's pawn sacrifice. Otherwise ...c5xd4 causes White's center to collapse.

8...Nc6   9.Be2 Bg4
This is Black's key resource. He is trying to unlock the potential of his g7-Bishop.

10.cxd6 exd6   11.exd6 Nxd6
The center has been blown up and White has won a pawn. The position shown in Diagram 225 offers Black excellent compensation.

Austrian Attack (6.Bd3)

This line and the next one are White's preferred choices in the Austrian Attack, as White plays for development (1.e4 d6 2.d4 Nf6 3.Nc3 g6 4.f4 Bg7 5.Nf3 O-O):

6.Bd3 Na6
A surprising move away from the center leads us to Diagram 226. Black supports his freeing break ...c7-c5, and once again invites e4-e5 by White.

7.O-O

226

White brings his King into safety before pressing in the center. White has tried playing for central control with 7.e5 Ne8 8.Be3. Black should persevere and prepare his central break ...c7-c5 by 8...b6. Black is not playing to fianchetto his Bishop; rather, he intends to smash White's center with ...c7-c5. Although White has a position that would make a classical player happy, Black's central counter will give him good play.

7...c5

Black goes for his standard break in the Austrian Attack. Grandmaster practice has shown that White's best chance for the advantage is to push his d-pawn.

8.d5 Rb8

The position is now similar to a Benoni, with Black playing for the ...b7-b5 push.

9.Kh1

This move is considered best as White sidesteps a number of tricks based upon ...b7-b5 and ...c5-c4. The immediate attacking plan, 9.Qe1 Nb4, gives Black the chance to win the two Bishops.

| **9...Nc7** | **10.a4 a6** |
| **11.a5 b5** | **12.axb6 Rxb6** |

As shown in Diagram 227, White has an advantage in the center, while Black's pressure is on the Queenside. He will play for ...Nc7-b5 and, in most cases, ...e7-e6, continuing to chip away at the center. The position is a highly charged one, typical of Benoni and Pirc Defenses. The chances are about even.

DIAGRAM 227.

Austrian Attack (6.Be3)

As in the previous lines of the Austrian Attack, White develops while retaining his central options (1.e4 d6 2.d4 Nf6 3.Nc3 g6 4.f4 Bg7 5.Nf3 O-O):

6.Be3

The advantage of this move is that it makes it much more difficult for Black to make his freeing ...c7-c5 break.

6...b6

Black spends an extra tempo preparing his ...c7-c5 break.

7.e5 Ng4

Usually the Knight parks itself on the e8-square. Black decides on the text to pick up a tempo.

8.Bg1 c5   9.h3

Black suffers the consequences of venturing forward. The Knight is forced into a retreat, but White spends a lot of time trying to corral the Knight.

9...Nh6 10.d5

It would be a mistake to play 10.dxc5? bxc5 11.Qd5? (trying to spear the Rook) because 11...Qb6! is excellent for Black. White tries to keep his center intact.

DIAGRAM 228.

10...Nd7

Provocative as ever, Black tries to lure White's center forward to its death.

11.Qe2

White protects the e5-pawn. After 11.e6? fxe6 12.dxe6 Nf6 13.Bc4 Nh5, Black wins the f4-pawn.

Diagram 228 shows the current position.

11...b5

In a beautifully timed break, Black attempts to kick away the only defender of the d-pawn.

12.O-O-O

The game is about to become violent as both Kings now face fierce attacks. 12.Nxb5 (12.Qxb5? Rb8 advantageously regains the b-pawn) 12...Qa5+ 13.Qd2 (13.c3 Ba6 and 13.Nc3 Rb8 both offer Black good compensation for the sacrificed pawn) 13...Qxd2+ 14.Kxd2 dxe5 results in approximate equality.

12...b4   13.Ne4 Nb6

14.g4 Bb7

The position shown in Diagram 229 is a barn burner, with both players having their trumps.

Pirc Defense (4.f3 or 4.Be3)

Building a house is a well-respected defensive strategy in grandmaster circles. For this reason, many players immediately try to storm the foundations by trading off the fianchettoed Bishop. After (1.e4 d6 2.d4 Nf6 3.Nc3 g6), Black has committed himself to the fianchetto. The favored move for White to trade the f8-Bishop is:

4.Be3

White wants to play Qd1-d2, Be3-h6, and probably h2-h4-h5, with a Kingside initiative. In the past, theorists suggested that White should preface the move with 4.f3, thereby preventing a timely ...Nf6-g4. Indeed, f2-f3 forms an important nucleus of White's plans, but this move should be delayed. White's point is that 4...Ng4 5.Bg5 h6 6.Bh4 g5 7.Bg3 sends Black on a wild goose chase.

DIAGRAM 229.

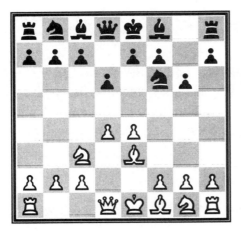

DIAGRAM 230.

He has weakened his Kingside without trading Knight for Bishop. The rule of thumb is that this kind of chase should be encouraged only if Black is able to nab the Bishop.

Diagram 230 shows the current position, in which Black must become a little crafty himself.

4...c6

Black makes an exception to the traditional "automatic" play to complete his house, 4...Bg7. The reason for the text is that Black anticipates that White will castle Queenside. He wants to save the tempo ...Bf8-g7 and accelerate a Queenside pawn storm.

5.Qd2 b5

Black reveals his point. He now threatens ...b5-b4, thereby chasing away the c3-Knight, the only defender of the e4-pawn.

6.f3

White reinforces his center. Although the moves 4.Be3 and 4.f3 are interchangeable, both players should be precise with their move order. Under the present order of moves, Black has forced White to include the tempo f2-f3. Without this order of moves, White might have foregone f2-f3 altogether. One of the benefits of f2-f3 is that White can now plan g2-g4-g5, removing an important defender with tempo. Again, Black should resist the temptation to automatically fianchetto his Bishop.

6...Nbd7   7.O-O-O

White has also tried to delay this committed move by 7.Nh3, 7.h4, 7.Bh6, and 7.g4, amongst others. 7.g4 aims for g4-g5; after 7...Nb6, Black has made room on the d7-square for his f6-Knight to retreat. That's why Black's opening move order deserves careful scrutiny.

7...Nb6

Diagram 231 shows the position.

Both players will zealously attempt to maul one another's King. A sample line might run:

8.g4 b4	**9.Nb1 a5**
10.h4 h5	**11.g5 Nh7**
12.Bd3 Bg7	

This leaves a wild game in view, featuring a typical Pirc middle game.

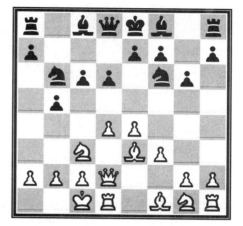

DIAGRAM 231.

Modern System

The lines described in the previous section gave a number of grandmasters some clever ideas, including (1.e4 d6 2.d4 Nf6 3.Nc3 g6):

4.Bg5

White reasons that he wants to play as before, using Qd1-d2 and Be3-h6 with a nice twist. He can also play for the Austrian Attack with the Bishop on a much more aggressive square.

4...h6

Black puts the question to the Bishop immediately. White would have an advantage after 4...Bg7 5.f4!, when the move e4-e5 will come with added punch because the g5-Bishop does so much more than in the previous Austrian Attack variations.

5.Be3

The position shown in Diagram 232 is nearly the same as the one shown in Diagram 230, with an important

DIAGRAM 232.

nuance: White has induced the move …h7-h6. The great debate is, which side benefits? It is clear that after the battery Qd1-d2, the h6-pawn is a target and Black's King is stuck in the center. Furthermore, White will be able to play g2-g4, h2-h4 and with g4-g5 insure himself of prying open the Kingside. On the other hand, White has robbed himself of the Be3-h6 trading Bishops option.

5…c6   6.f3 b5
7.Qd2 Nbd7

After these moves, the game is similar to the previous variation with the h6-pawn sticking out. Black's King shouldn't be too uncomfortable in the center because White isn't threatening to crash through any time soon.

Pirc Defense (4.Be2)

A rather cunning line is (1.e4 d6 2.d4 Nf6 3.Nc3 g6):

4.Be2

White has not revealed his point. He might easily transpose into the main line, which I describe later in this chapter.

4…Bg7   5.h4

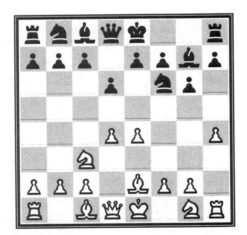

DIAGRAM 233.

Diagram 233 shows White's belligerent move. It's appalling that White decides to storm the house before the Black King even makes it to the Kingside. White's intentions are as clear as they are aggressive. He will push his h-pawn and rip open the Kingside. It would now be a grievous error for Black to play 5…O-O, for as they say in chess parlance, "Black would castle into it." And by *it*, they mean a bone-crunching attack. After

White's fifth move, Black should definitely be put off from castling Kingside for awhile.

5...c5

Once more Black strikes in the center with this familiar counter. This brings me to the last wise opening principle of this book:

An attack on the wing is best met by a counter in the center.

This dictum was laid down centuries ago and it's as valid as ever. Time and time again in master games you will see this type of principled response. Look for it in your games too.

Black forces a central response.

6.dxc5

White could try 6.d5 a6 7.h5 (7.a4 e6 leaves White wondering where he will castle) 7...b5, which produces the better position for Black.

6...Qa5

Black utilizes a standard Pirc Defense resource, and threatens ...Nf6xe4 with advantage.

7.Qd3

White defends the e4-pawn and sets a cunning trap: 7...Nxe4?? 8.Qb5+ wins a piece.

7...Qxc5   8.Be3 Qa5
9.h5

White pursues his Kingside play.

9...Nc6 10.h6

White achieves nothing from 10.hxg6 hxg6 11.Rxh8+ Bxh8, when Black has a fine position.

10...Bf8   11.O-O-O Bd7

As shown in Diagram 234, the position has become an unusual Sicilian where Black has an excellent game.

DIAGRAM 234.

233

Geller Quiet System (Pirc Defense Main Line)

Russian Grandmaster Efim Geller is a first-class attacker of the highest order. He is one of the few players in the world to have a better score against Bobby Fischer. When such a bold player devises a "quiet" line against the Pirc Defense, you just know that things are boiling below the surface. Play begins with a fundamentally principled move in which White develops his Knight to its best square (1.e4 d6 2.d4 Nf6 3.Nc3 g6):

4.Nf3 Bg7   5.Be2 O-O

6.O-O

Diagram 235 shows the starting position of Geller's system. White has a classical pawn center and is happy with his gain. It is up to Black to find an effective counter.

6...c6

With this multipurpose move, Black feints a possible ...b7-b5, but mainly intends to cover the d5-square. In some lines, Black can also play ...d6-d5 intending to leap into the e4-square. White has tried three plans:

- 7.a4 prevents a possible ...b7-b5 Queenside expansion
- 7.h3 prevents a possible ...Bc8-g4 while making luft (that is, he creates "air" for his King)
- 7.Re1 supports his center and prepares e4-e5

Geller Quiet System (7.a4)

While this move reasonably furthers White's intention of preventing a Queenside expansion, it hardly pressures Black's position (1.e4 d6 2.d4 Nf6 3.Nc3 g6 4.Nf3 Bg7 5.Be2 O-O 6.O-O c6):

7.a4 Nbd7

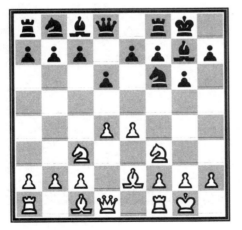

DIAGRAM 235.

As shown in Diagram 236, Black is aiming for the traditional ...e7-e5 counter.

8.Be3 e5   **9.dxe5 dxe5**
10.Qd6 Re8   **11.Bc4**

White targets the f7-pawn.

11...Qe7   **12.Rad1 Qxd6**
13.Rxd6 Bf8!

Black forces the Rook away with tempo.

14.Rdd1

White's Rook has an uncomfortable time finding a good square on the d-file.

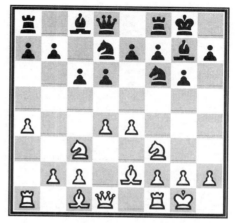

DIAGRAM 236.

14...Kg7

I prefer Black's position.

Geller Quiet System (7.h3)

This is a far more useful move. White makes luft and prevents annoyances from happening on the g4-square, by (1.e4 d6 2.d4 Nf6 3.Nc3 g6 4.Nf3 Bg7 5.Be2 O-O 6.O-O c6):

7.h3

White also is set to play 8.e5 dxe5 9.dxe5, forcing the f6-Knight to retreat.

7...Nbd7

Black concedes that ...b7-b5 is not yet a threat. Black stands badly after: 7...b5 8.e5 dxe5 9.Nxe5, when Be2-f3 gives White strong pressure.

8.e5

Otherwise Black will play ...e7-e5. Kasparov as Black has faced 8.Bf4 Qa5 9.Qd2 e5 10.dxe5 dxe5 11.Bh6 Re8 and soon got the better game.

Diagram 237, on the next page, shows the current position.

8...Ne8

235

DIAGRAM 237.

This standard retreat is much better than 8...Nd5?! 9.Nxd5 cxd5 10.exd6 exd6, when White has the better game due to the pawn structure.

9.Re1 dxe5   10.dxe5 Nc7!

Black's Knight finds a different way to liberate itself.

11.Bf1 Ne6

The position is considered equal as White has problems creating active play in the center.

Geller Quiet System (7.Re1)

This is the most dangerous line for Black. White supports his e-pawn so that it will act as a bowling ball as it moves up the board, knocking pieces out of the way (1.e4 d6 2.d4 Nf6 3.Nc3 g6 4.Nf3 Bg7 5.Be2 O-O 6.O-O c6):

7.Re1 Nbd7   8.Bf4

Diagram 238 shows the most trying position that Black faces in the Pirc Defense today.

8...Qc7

Black is ready to make his central ...e7-e5 break forcing White's response:

9.e5 Nh5   10.exd6 exd6
11.Bg5 Re8

Black is kicking well. He is prepared to play ...Nd7-b6 and develop the rest of his forces.

I hope, dear reader, that you have enjoyed *Winning Chess Open-*

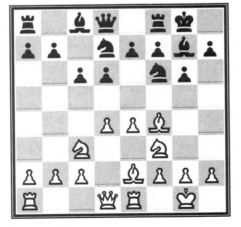

DIAGRAM 238.

ings, and that it has given you some insight into classical and modern openings and defenses. I hope that my recommended formations of the Barcza Opening, the King's Indian Defense, and the Pirc Defense will bring you a career of success as they have brought me. Happy hunting.

Glossary

Active: An aggressive move or position.

Advantage: A net superiority of position, usually based on force, time, space, or pawn structure.

Algebraic Notation: The international standard for writing chess moves. Each square on the chessboard is given a letter and a number, as shown in Diagram 239.

When a piece travels from one square to another, algebraic notation enables you to identify the piece and the square to which it is moving. For example, if the Rook moves from square a1 to square a8, you write Ra8. For pawn moves, you write only the square to which the pawn moves; for example, e4. Castling Kingside is written O-O, and castling Queenside is written O-O-O.

Analysis: The calculation of a series of moves based on a particular position. In tournament play, you are not allowed to move the pieces during analysis but must make all calculations in your head. When the game is over, opponents commonly analyze the game they have just played, moving the pieces about in an effort to discover what the best moves would have been.

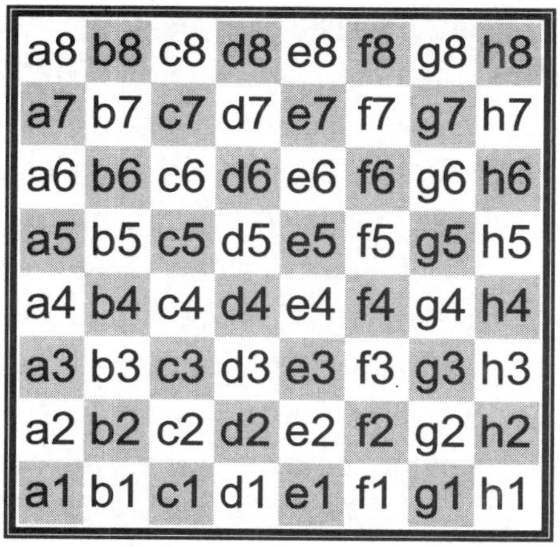

a8	b8	c8	d8	e8	f8	g8	h8
a7	b7	c7	d7	e7	f7	g7	h7
a6	b6	c6	d6	e6	f6	g6	h6
a5	b5	c5	d5	e5	f5	g5	h5
a4	b4	c4	d4	e4	f4	g4	h4
a3	b3	c3	d3	e3	f3	g3	h3
a2	b2	c2	d2	e2	f2	g2	h2
a1	b1	c1	d1	e1	f1	g1	h1

DIAGRAM 239.

Attack: To start an aggressive action in a particular area of the board, or to threaten to capture a piece or pawn.

Bind: When one player has a grip on the position because of a large advantage in space and his opponent is unable to find useful moves.

Bishop Pair: Two Bishops versus a Bishop and a Knight or two Knights. Two Bishops work well together because they can control diagonals of both colors. *See also* Opposite-Colored Bishops.

Blockade: To stop an enemy pawn by placing a piece (ideally a Knight) directly in front of it. Popularized by Aaron Nimzovitch.

Blunder: A terrible move that loses material or involves decisive positional or tactical concessions.

Book: Opening analysis found in chess books and magazines. A *book player* relies heavily on memorization of published material rather than on his own creative spark.

Break: The offer of an exchange of pawns in order to gain space or mobility. Also called a *pawn break*.

Castle: A player castles by moving his King and Rook simultaneously. Castling is the only move in which a player can deploy two pieces in one move. Castling allows a player to move his King out of the center (the main theater of action in the opening) to the flank, where the King can be protected by pawns. Additionally, castling develops a Rook.

When White castles Kingside, he moves his King from e1 to g1 and his h1-Rook to f1. When Black castles Kingside, he moves his King from e8 to g8 and his h8-Rook to f8. When White castles Queenside, he moves his King from e1 to c1 and his a1-Rook to d1. And when Black castles Queenside, he moves his King from e8 to c8 and his a8-Rook to d8.

Center: The center is the area of the board encompassed by the rectangle c3-c6-f6-f3. Squares e4, d4, e5, and d5 are the most important part of the center. The e- and d-files are the *center files*.

Centralize: To place pieces or pawns in the center, or as close to the center as possible. From there, they can control a good chunk of enemy territory.

Checkmate: An attack against the enemy King from which the King cannot escape. When a player checkmates his opponent's King, he wins the game.

Classical: A style of play that focuses on the creation of a full pawn center. Classical principles tend to be rather dogmatic and inflexible. The philosophy of the classical players was eventually challenged by the so-called "hypermoderns." *See also* Hypermodern.

Closed Game: A position that is obstructed by blocking chains of pawns. Such a position tends to favor Knights over Bishops, because the pawns block the diagonals.

Combination: A sacrifice combined with a forced series of moves, which exploits specific peculiarities of the positions in the hope of attaining a certain goal.

Compensation: An advantage in one area that balances the opponent's advantage in another area. Material versus development is one example; three pawns versus a Bishop is another.

Control: To completely dominate an area of the board. Dominating a file or a square, or simply having the initiative, can constitute control.

Counterplay: When the player who has been on the defensive starts his own aggressive action.

Cramp: The lack of mobility that is usually the result of a disadvantage in space.

Critical Position: An important point in the game, where victory or defeat hangs in the balance.

Defense: A move or series of moves designed to thwart an enemy attack. Also used in the names of many openings initiated by Black. Examples are the French Defense and the Caro-Kann Defense.

Development: The process of moving pieces from their starting positions to new posts, from which they control a greater number of squares and have greater mobility.

Discovered Attack: A discovered attack is an ambush. A Queen, Rook, or Bishop lies in wait so that it can attack when another piece or pawn moves out of its way.

Discovered Check: The most effective type of discovered attack, which involves checking the enemy King.

Double Attack: An attack against two pieces or pawns at the same time.

Double Check: The most powerful type of discovered attack, which checks the King with two pieces. The King is forced to move, and the enemy army is thus frozen for at least one move.

Doubled Pawns: Two pawns of the same color lined up on a file. This doubling can only come about as the result of a capture.

Draw: A tied game. A draw can result from a stalemate, from a three-time repetition of position, or by agreement between the players.

Dynamic: Implies action and movement. A dynamic factor concerns itself with actual moves and threats and involves combinations of attack and defense maneuvers. The two main aspects of a dynamic factor are time and force.

Endgame: The third and final phase of a chess game. An endgame arises when few pieces remain on the board. The clearest signal that the ending is about to begin is when Queens are exchanged.

En Prise: A French term that means *in take*. It describes a piece or pawn that is vulnerable to capture.

Equality: A situation in which neither side has an advantage or the players' advantages balance out.

Exchange: The trading of pieces, usually pieces of equal value.

Exchange, The: *Winning the Exchange* means winning a Rook for a Bishop or a Knight.

Fianchetto: An Italian term that means *on the flank* and applies only to Bishops. A fianchetto (pronounced *fyan-KET-to*) involves placing a White Bishop on g2 or b2 or a Black Bishop on g7 or b7.

FIDE: The acronym for *Fédération Internationale des Échecs*, the international chess federation.

File: A vertical column of eight squares. Designated in algebraic notation as the a-file, b-file, and so on. *See also* Half-Open File; Open File.

Flank: The a-, b-, and c-files on the Queenside, and the f-, g-, and h-files on the Kingside.

Force: An advantage in force arises when one player has more material than his opponent or when he outmans his opponent in a certain area of the board.

Forced: A move or series of moves that must be played if disaster is to be avoided.

Fork: A tactical maneuver in which a piece or pawn attacks two enemy pieces or pawns at the same time.

Gambit: The voluntary sacrifice of at least a pawn in the opening, with the idea of gaining a compensating advantage (usually time, which permits development).

Grandmaster: A title awarded by FIDE to players who meet an established set of performance standards, including a high rating. It is the highest title (other than World Champion) attainable in chess. Lesser titles include International Master and FIDE Master, which is the lowest title awarded for international play. Once earned, a Grandmaster title cannot be taken away. *See also* Master.

Half-Open File: A file that contains none of one player's pawns but one or more of his opponent's.

Hanging Pawns: A pawn island consisting of two pawns side by side on the 4th rank on half-open files. Sometimes, hanging pawns are the source of dynamic energy for an attack; at other times, they become a target, subject to frontal attack by the enemy. *See also* Pawn Island.

Hypermodern: A school of thought that arose in reaction to the classical theories of chess. The hypermoderns insisted that putting a pawn in the center in the opening made it a target. The heroes of this movement were Richard Réti and Aaron Nimzovich, both of whom expounded the idea of controlling the center from the flanks. Like the ideas of the classicists, those of the hypermoderns can be carried to extremes. Nowadays, both views are seen as correct. A distillation of the two philosophies is needed to cope successfully with any particular situation. *See also* Classical.

Initiative: When you are able to make threats to which your opponent must react, you are said to *possess the initiative.*

Isolated Pawn: A pawn with no like-colored pawns on either adjacent file. The drawbacks of an isolated pawn are that it is not guarded by a friendly pawn and that the square directly in front of it can make a nice home for an enemy piece, because no pawns can chase that piece away. On the other hand, an isolated pawn has plenty of space and controls squares on the open (or half-open) files on either side of it, with the result that minor pieces and Rooks of the same color usually become active. An isolated pawn is, however, considered a weakness.

Kingside: The half of the board made up of the e, f, g, and h files. Kingside pieces are the King, the Bishop next to it, the Knight next to the Bishop, and the Rook next to the Knight. *See also* Queenside.

Luft: A German term that means *air.* In chess, it means *to give the King breathing room.* It describes a pawn move made in front of the King of the same color to avoid back rank mate possibilities.

Major Pieces: Queens and Rooks. Also called *heavy pieces.*

Master: In the US, a player with a rating of 2200 or more. If a player's rating drops below 2200, the title is rescinded. *See also* Grandmaster.

Mate: Short for *checkmate.*

Material: All the pieces and pawns. A *material advantage* is when a player has more pieces on the board than his opponent or has pieces of greater value.

Mating Attack: An attack on the enemy King, with checkmate as the ultimate goal.

Middle Game: The phase between the opening and the endgame.

Minor Pieces: The Bishops and Knights.

Mobility: Freedom of movement for the pieces.

Occupation: A Rook or Queen that controls a file or rank is said to *occupy* that file or rank. A piece is said to occupy the square it is sitting on.

Open File: A vertical column of eight squares that is free of pawns. Rooks reach their maximum potential when placed on open files or open ranks.

Open Game: A position characterized by many open ranks, files, or diagonals and few center pawns. A lead in development becomes very important in positions of this type.

Opening: The start of a game, incorporating the first dozen or so moves. The basic goals of an opening are to:

- Develop pieces as quickly as possible
- Control as much of the center as possible
- Castle early and get the King to safety, while at the same time bringing the Rooks toward the center and placing them on potentially open files

Openings: Established sequences of moves that lead to the goals outlined under Opening. These sequences of moves are often named after the player who invented them or after the place where they were first played. Some openings, such as the *King's Gambit* and the *English*, have been analyzed to great lengths in chess literature.

Opposite-Colored Bishops: Also *Bishops of opposite color.* When players have one Bishop each and the Bishops are on different-colored squares. Opposite-colored Bishops can never come into direct contact.

Overextension: When space is gained too fast. By rushing his pawns forward and trying to control a lot of territory, a player can leave weaknesses in his camp, or can weaken the advanced pawns themselves. He is then said to have *overextended* his position.

Passive: In relation to a move, denotes a move that does nothing to fight for the initiative. In relation to a position, denotes a position that is devoid of counterplay or active possibilities.

Pawn Center: Pawns that are inside the rectangle bounded by squares c3, f3, f6, and c6.

Pawn Chain: A diagonal line of same-colored pawns.

Pawn Island: Two pawns are members of different islands if neither can protect the other. Pawn islands are separated by open files. Pawns that are both doubled and isolated constitute two pawn islands. Having fewer pawn islands than the opponent is advantageous. *See also* Hanging Pawns.

Pawn Structure: Also referred to as the *pawn skeleton*. All aspects of the pawn setup.

Perpetual Check: When one player places his opponent in check, forcing a reply, followed by another check and another forced reply, followed by another check that repeats the first position. Because such a game could be played forever, after the position repeats itself, the game is declared a draw.

Pin: When one player attacks a piece that his opponent cannot move without losing a different piece of greater value. When the piece of greater value is the King, this tactic is called an *absolute pin*; when it is not the King, the tactic is called a *relative pin*.

Plan: A short- or long-range goal on which a player bases his moves.

Poisoned Pawn: A pawn whose capture is a precursor to a strong attack.

Positional: A move or style of play that is based on long-range consider-ations. The slow buildup of small advantages is said to be positional.

Premature: Taking action without sufficient preparation.

Prepared Variation: In professional chess, it is common practice to analyze book openings in the hope of finding a new move or plan. When a player makes such a discovery, he will often save this prepared variation for use against a special opponent.

Queenside: The half of the board that includes the d-, c-, b-, and a-files. The Queenside pieces are the Queen, the Bishop next to it, the Knight next to the Bishop, and the Rook next to the Knight. *See also* Kingside.

Quiet Move: An unassuming move that is not a capture, a check, or a direct threat. A quiet move often occurs at the end of a maneuver or combination that drives the point home.

Rank: A horizontal row of eight squares. Designated in algebraic notation as the 1 (1st) rank, the 2 (2nd) rank, and so on.

Rating: A number that measures a player's relative strength. The higher the number, the stronger the player.

Resign: When a player realizes that he is going to lose and graciously gives up the game without waiting for a checkmate. When resigning, a player can simply say, "I resign," or he can tip over his King in a gesture of helplessness. When you first start playing chess, I recommend that you never resign. Always play until the end.

Sacrifice: The voluntary offer of material for compensation in space, time, pawn structure, or even force. (A sacrifice can lead to a force advantage in a particular part of the board.) Unlike a combination, a sacrifice is not always a calculable commodity and often entails an element of uncertainty.

Sharp: An aggressive move or position. In relation to a player, denotes someone who enjoys dynamic, attacking chess.

Skewer: A threat against a valuable piece that forces that piece to move, allowing the capture of a less valuable piece behind it.

Smothered Checkmate: When a King is completely surrounded by its own pieces (or is at the edge of the board) and it receives an unanswerable check from the enemy.

Space: The territory controlled by each player.

Speculative: Made without calculating the consequences to the extent normally required. Sometimes full calculation is not possible, so a player must rely on intuition, from which a speculative plan might arise.

Strategy: The reasoning behind a move, plan, or idea.

Tactics: Maneuvers that take advantage of short-term opportunities. A position with many traps and combinations is considered to be *tactical in nature.*

Tempo: One move, as a unit of time; the plural is *tempi.* If a piece can reach a useful square in one move but takes two moves to get there, it has lost a tempo. For example, after 1.e4 e5 2.d4 exd4 3.Qxd4 Nc6, Black gains a tempo and White loses one because the White Queen is attacked and White must move his Queen a second time to get it to safety.

Theory: Well-known opening, middle game, and endgame positions that are documented in books.

Transposition: Reaching an identical opening position by a different order of moves. For example, the French Defense is usually reached by 1.e4 e6 2.d4 d5, but 1.d4 e6 2.e4 d5 *transposes* into the same position.

Trap: A way of surreptitiously luring the opponent into making a mistake.

Two Bishops: *See* Bishop Pair.

Unclear: An assessment of a position. Some positions are good for White, others are good for Black, and still others are equal. Unclear means that the analyst is unable or unwilling to state which applies.

Variation: One line of analysis in any phase of the game. It could be a line of play other than the ones used in the game. The term *variation* is frequently applied to one line of an opening; for example, the Wilkes-Barre Variation (named after the city in Pennsylvania) of the Two Knights' Defense. Variations can become as well-analyzed as their parent openings. Entire books have been written on some well-known variations.

Weakness: Any pawn or square that is readily attackable and therefore hard to defend.

Index

Yasser Seirawan

International Chess Grandmaster Yasser Seirawan is one of the top U.S. contenders for the world championship title. He was the first American contender for the world title since Bobby Fischer retired in 1975. Seirawan qualified for the world championships in 1985, 1987, and 1997. He has earned numerous titles, including 1979 World Junior Champion, U.S. Champion (three times), and 1989 Western Hemisphere Champion, and he is a seven-time member of the U.S. Olympic chess team. In the 1994 Chess Olympics, he earned an individual gold medal for best individual score. He has defeated the two top-ranking players in the world, Garry Kasparov and Anatoly Karpov, in tournament play. He is the only American to have played in the World Cup cycle.

Born in Damascus, Syria, in 1960, Seirawan moved with his family to Seattle at the age of 7. His chess career was launched at the age of 12 when he began to play in local and regional tournaments. Seirawan lives in Seattle, Washington, where he is the publisher of *Inside Chess* magazine. He is the author of 11 books on chess, including the award-winning series published by Microsoft Press. Readers are invited to write to him at PO Box 19457, Seattle, WA 98109 to receive a free copy of *Inside Chess* magazine and a catalog of chess products.

In 1987, Seirawan founded International Chess Enterprises, Inc. (ICE), and he continues to serve as its President. ICE specializes in publishing chess books, magazines, and software through traditional means and on the Internet. In 1992, ICE became a publicly traded company on the Vancouver Stock Exchange and is traded as Masterpiece Games Inc. (MPA:VSE).